Cambridge Essentials

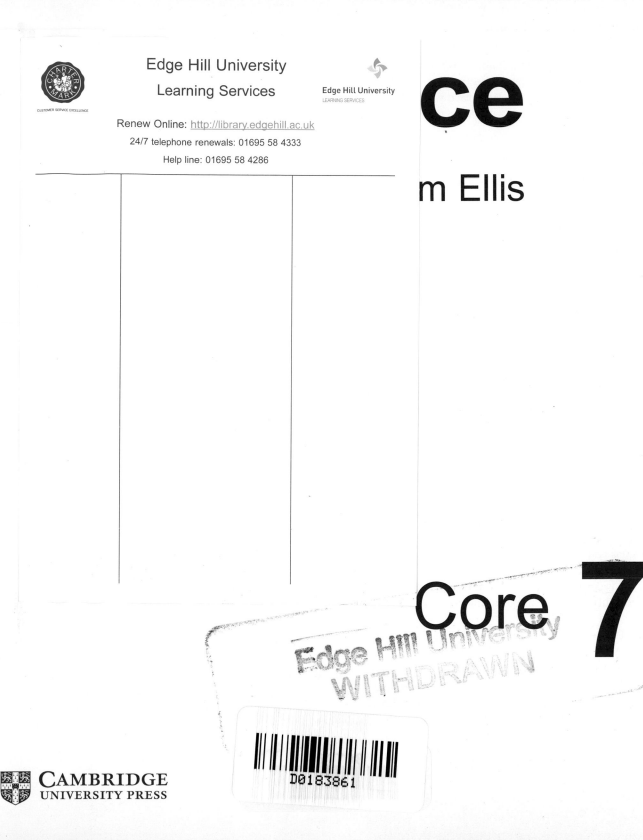

Science

Sam Ellis

Core 7

CAMBRIDGE
UNIVERSITY PRESS

CAMBRIDGE UNIVERSITY PRESS
Cambridge, New York, Melbourne, Madrid, Cape Town, Singapore,
São Paulo, Delhi

Cambridge University Press
The Edinburgh Building, Cambridge CB2 8RU, UK

www.cambridge.org
Information on this title: www.cambridge.org/9780521725675

First published 2008

Book printed in the United Kingdom at the University Press, Cambridge

A catalogue record for this publication is available from the British Library

ISBN 978-0-521-72567-5 paperback with CD-ROM

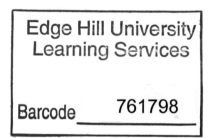

Contents

Introduction

Take advantage of the CD

Cambridge Essentials Science comes with a CD in the back. This contains the entire book as an interactive PDF file, which you can read on your computer using free Adobe Reader software from Adobe (www.adobe.com/products/acrobat/readstep2.html). As well as the material you can see in the book, the PDF file gives you extras when you click on the buttons you will see on most pages; see the inside front cover for a brief explanation of these.

To use the CD, simply insert it into the CD or DVD drive of your computer. You will be prompted to install the contents of the CD to your hard drive. Installing will make it easier to use the PDF file, because the installer creates an icon on your desktop that launches the PDF directly. However, it will run just as well straight from the CD.

If you want to install the contents of the disc onto your hard disc yourself, this is easily done. Just open the disc contents in your file manager (for Apple Macs, double click on the CD icon on your desktop; for Windows, open My Computer and double click on your CD drive icon), select all the files and folders and copy them wherever you want.

Take advantage of the web

Cambridge Essentials Science lets you go directly from your book to web-based activities on our website, including animations, exercises, investigations and quizzes. Access is free to all users of the book.

There are three kinds of activity, each linked to from a different place within each unit.

- **Scientific enquiry:** these buttons appear at the start and end of each unit. The activities in this section allow you to develop skills related to scientific enquiry, including experiments that would be hard to carry out in the classroom.

- **Check your progress:** these buttons come half-way through each unit. They let you check how well you have understood the unit so far.

- **Review your work:** these buttons come at the end of each unit. They let you show that you have understood the unit, or let you find areas where you need more work.

The *Teacher Material* CD-ROM for *Cambridge Essentials Science* contains enhanced interactive PDFs. As well as all the features of the pupil PDF, teachers have links to the *Essentials Science* Planner – a new website with a full lesson planning tool, including worksheets, practicals, assessment materials, guidance and example lesson plans. The e-learning materials are fully integrated, letting you see the animations in context and alongside all the other materials.

7A.1 What living things are made from (HSW)

Aristotle lived in Greece over 2000 years ago. He was very interested in plants and animals and in how the human body works.

Look at the drawing by Aristotle of some parts of the human body.

We call these parts **organs**. Old drawings and texts from China and the Middle East also show human organs. Some even show plant organs.

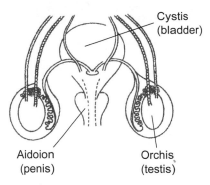

Aristotle's drawing.

At first, information about human organs came from

- operations
- cutting up dead bodies.

Now we can look at X-rays and body scans, too.

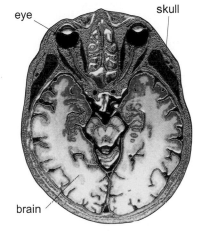

A scan through part of the head.

Question 1 / 2

A closer look at human organs

In the late 18th century, a French doctor called Xavier Bichat did hundreds of post-mortems. Post-mortems are operations carried out on dead bodies to find out what killed them.

Bichat found that each human organ contains more than one kind of material. He listed 21 different kinds. We call these materials **tissues**. Bichat couldn't see the detailed structure of these tissues because he didn't have a microscope.

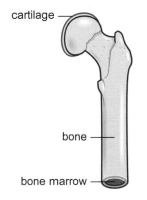

Part of a thigh bone.

Question 3 / 4

7A Cells: the body's building blocks   1

| You should already know | Outcomes | Keywords |

Microscopes were invented in the 16th century but their lenses were not very good.

Type of microscope	Invented by	About the images
simple (1 lens)		not very clear
compound (2 lenses)	Hans and Zacharias Janssen (Dutch) in 1590 and later by Robert Hooke (English)	better images
simple (1 lens – but a better one)	Antonie van Leeuwenhoek (Dutch) in 1673	even better – things looked 200 times larger than they really were

Some of the first microscopes.

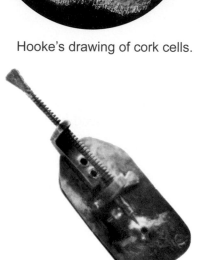

Hooke's drawing of cork cells.

1665 Hooke published his drawings of microscopic structures. One of the drawings was of a slice of cork. It showed that cork is made up of what look like tiny boxes. He called these boxes **cells**.

1683 Leeuwenhoek published his drawings of microscopic creatures. Because his lens was so much better, the images were clearer than Hooke's. He could see more details.

1831 A Scot, Robert Brown, saw and named the **nucleus**.

1840 German scientists, Matthias Schleiden and Theodor Schwann, published the <u>cell theory</u> – that all plants and animals are made of cells.

Leeuwenhoek's microscope.

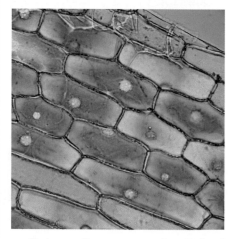

Onion cells as seen using Robert Brown's microscope.

Question 1 | 2 | 3

Scale drawings

When we draw what we see under a microscope, we draw things much bigger than they really are. We draw them to **scale**.

We often use scale drawings in our lives, not just in science.

Maps and plans are scale diagrams. They show places smaller than they really are. We call this <u>scaling down</u>.

When we show things bigger than they really are, we are <u>scaling up</u>.

You can show a scale in one of these ways:

×20 |—— 1 mm ——|

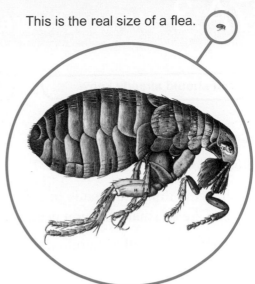

This is the real size of a flea.

Robert Hooke drew a flea bigger than it really is. This means you can see more detail.

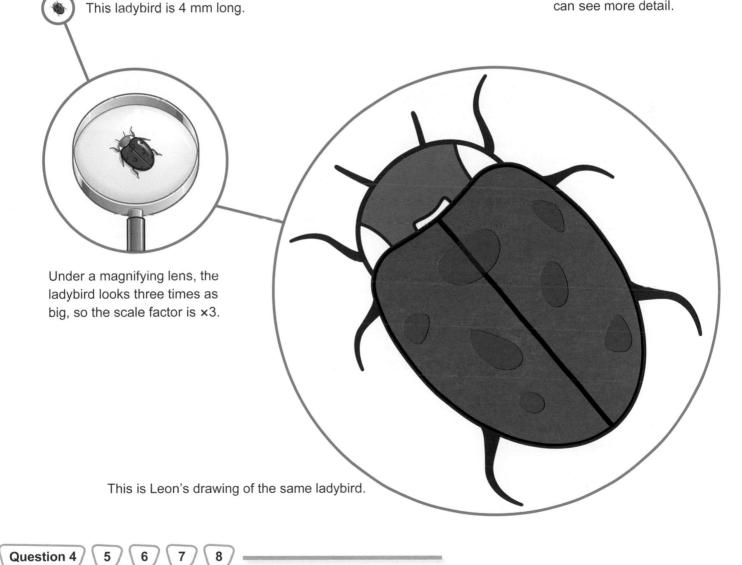

This ladybird is 4 mm long.

Under a magnifying lens, the ladybird looks three times as big, so the scale factor is ×3.

This is Leon's drawing of the same ladybird.

Question 4 5 6 7 8

You should already know	Outcomes	Keywords

Cells are very small

Remember that

- all living things are made of cells
- cells are so small that you need a microscope to see them.

If you magnify cells a hundred times or more, you can see smaller parts inside them.

Non-living things show different types of structure.
Sometimes there is no detail to see under a light microscope.

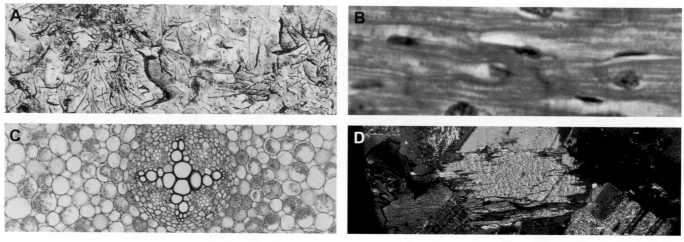

Four microscope views of living and non-living things.

> **Question 1**

Cells are not all alike

All cells are very small. But they are not all the same size.

In this square, □, you could fit

- 2500 rhubarb skin cells, or
- 10 000 human skin cells.

Cells also vary in shape.

Plant and animal cells look quite different under the microscope.

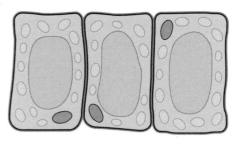

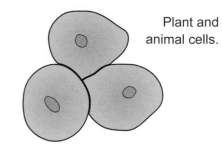

Plant and animal cells.

> **Question 2**

A closer look at animal cells

Cells are made of lots of different parts.

Each part has a different job to do to keep the cell

- alive
- working properly.

Chris scraped some cells from the skin inside her cheek.

Cheek cells.

Under the microscope the cells look coloured. The colour is a stain that makes them show up more clearly.

I control what happens in the cell.

nucleus

I'm like jelly. Most of the chemical reactions happen inside me.

cytoplasm

cell membrane

I'm very thin. I let things pass in and out of the cell.

Question 3 / **4**

Plant cells aren't quite the same

Chris also made a slide of a moss leaf.

She looked at the cells under a microscope.

Cells in a moss leaf.

A moss plant.

I use light energy to make food for the plant. I am only in cells in the green parts of plants.

cytoplasm
nucleus
chloroplast
cell membrane

I'm full of liquid cell sap. I store water, salts and sugars.

vacuole

cell wall

I'm strong and I help the plant cell to keep its shape.

Question 5 / **6**

You should already know

Outcomes

Keywords

There are over a million different types of animal. They all have different shapes and sizes.

But in all these animals there are only about 200 different kinds of cell. These cells are different because they do <u>different</u> jobs. The cells on the inside of the breathing tubes of humans and other animals are similar because they do the <u>same</u> jobs.

	Goblet cells	**Ciliated epithelial cells**
Called this because...	of their shape	cilia = beating hairs epithelium = skin or lining
Job	to make sticky mucus to trap dust and micro-organisms	to carry the mucus out of the lungs

Two kinds of cells in breathing tube linings.

Question 1

More specialised cells

Nerve cells are very long. Your brain and spinal cord send and receive messages in the form of nerve impulses from all over your body.

Your **red blood cells** are full of a chemical called haemoglobin. This can join with oxygen. So your blood can carry oxygen to every cell in the body.

Plants have special cells too. **Root hair cells** are one example. The hairs give the roots a bigger surface for absorbing water.

Question 2 **3** **4**

How cells work together

A house doesn't look like a living thing! However, the way the building materials of a house are grouped is similar to the way that cells in a living thing are organised.

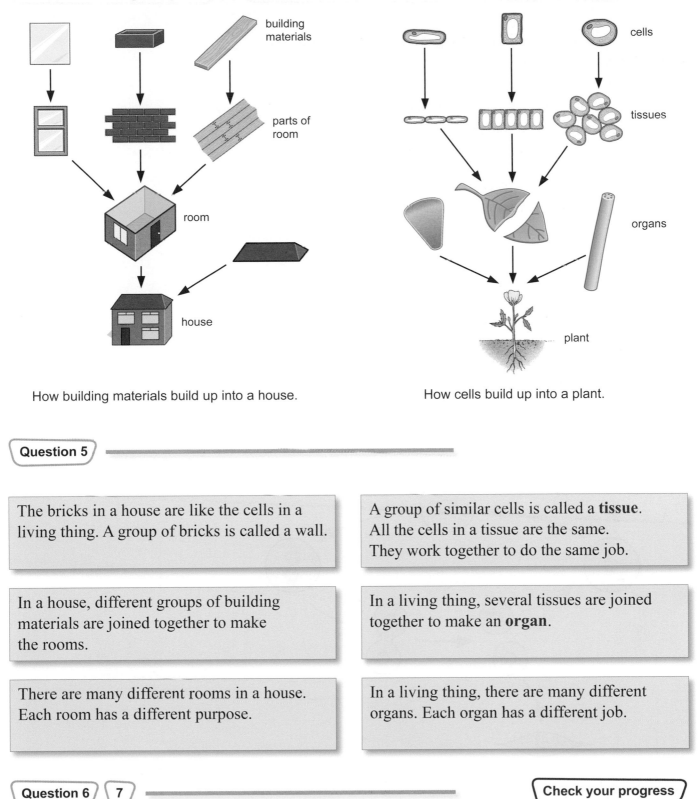

How building materials build up into a house.

How cells build up into a plant.

Question 5

The bricks in a house are like the cells in a living thing. A group of bricks is called a wall.	A group of similar cells is called a **tissue**. All the cells in a tissue are the same. They work together to do the same job.
In a house, different groups of building materials are joined together to make the rooms.	In a living thing, several tissues are joined together to make an **organ**.
There are many different rooms in a house. Each room has a different purpose.	In a living thing, there are many different organs. Each organ has a different job.

Question 6 **7** **Check your progress**

You should already know

Outcomes

Keywords

People used to think that living things sometimes appeared out of nowhere.

- They saw maggots appear in rotting meat.
- Leeuwenhoek described tiny living animals in rotting things.

So the idea seemed to be sensible.

In the 19th century, Louis Pasteur proved that this idea was wrong. He showed that living things come only from other living things.

Cells don't just appear from nowhere either.

In 1858, a German scientist called Rudolph Virchow suggested that new cells could only grow from cells that were already there.

Now we know that new cells form only when cells divide.

Question 1

How a cell divides

The nucleus divides first and then the cell. As the new cells take in more materials, they grow. When they are big enough, the cells divide again. We call this the **cell cycle**.

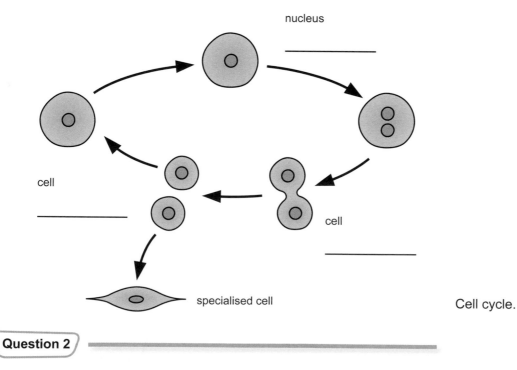

nucleus

cell

cell

specialised cell

Cell cycle.

Question 2

Plant cell division

When a plant cell divides, it's not just the nucleus and cytoplasm that divide. A new cell wall forms between the new nuclei.

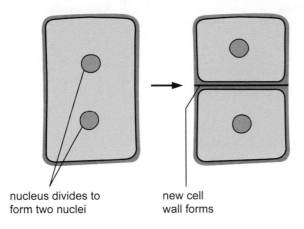

nucleus divides to form two nuclei

new cell wall forms

How a plant cell divides.

Specialised cells

Some cells divide over and over again, but other cells become specialised to do particular jobs. Specialised cells don't divide again.

Question 3

The nucleus controls how a cell develops

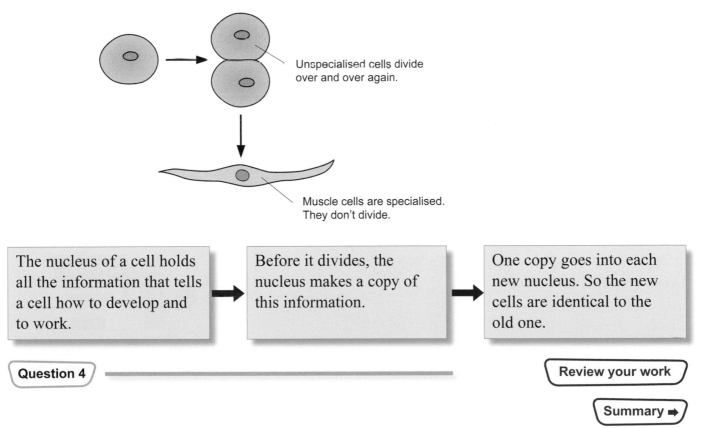

Unspecialised cells divide over and over again.

Muscle cells are specialised. They don't divide.

| The nucleus of a cell holds all the information that tells a cell how to develop and to work. | Before it divides, the nucleus makes a copy of this information. | One copy goes into each new nucleus. So the new cells are identical to the old one. |

Question 4

Review your work

Summary ➡

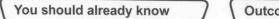
You should already know | Outcomes | Keywords

New evidence, new explanations

Just like detectives, scientists try to explain the **evidence** that they collect.

They suggest **theories** based on the evidence they have at the time.

With new evidence, they may change their ideas and suggest new theories.

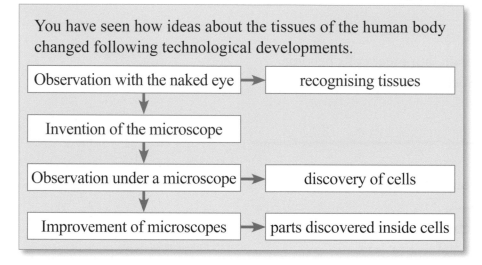

You have seen how ideas about the tissues of the human body changed following technological developments.

Observation with the naked eye → recognising tissues

↓

Invention of the microscope

↓

Observation under a microscope → discovery of cells

↓

Improvement of microscopes → parts discovered inside cells

Question 1

<u>17th and early 18th centuries</u> Lenses and microscopes improved.

<u>1886</u> German instrument manufacturer Carl Zeiss asked scientist Ernst Abbe to design a better microscope.

Abbe's microscopes are a bit like the ones you use.

They have two lenses, a stage and a mirror. Look back at Topic 7A.2 to see how different they are from Leeuwenhoek's microscope.

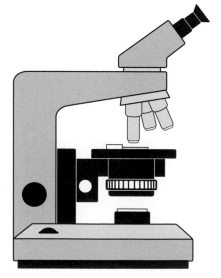

Light microscope.

What Zeiss and Abbe did

Zeiss asked Abbe to use <u>optics theory</u> to design a better microscope. Abbe's first microscopes didn't work very well. So he did <u>experiments</u> with lenses to find out what happens to light passing through lenses to form an image.

From his experiments, he was able

- to suggest a theory about how microscope images formed
- to test his theory by doing more experiments
- to put his theory into practice in his designs.

We study cells in <u>biology</u>.

We study light and optics in <u>physics</u>.

Applying science is <u>technology</u>.

The story of cells shows the importance of working together.

Scientists gather information by **observing** and **experimenting**.

They use the evidence to make theories, and then gather more evidence to test those theories.

Question 2 3

Abbe found that the properties of light limit what can be seen clearly using a light microscope. He predicted that future 'microscopes' might overcome this problem.

Magnifying even more

Abbe's prediction came true in 1931. German engineers Ernst Ruska and Max Knoll invented the first basic <u>electron microscope</u>. It used a beam of electrons, not a light beam.

With modern electron microscopes, we can now

- see much more detail inside cells.
- magnify objects up to two million times, which is 1000 times more than the very best light microscopes.

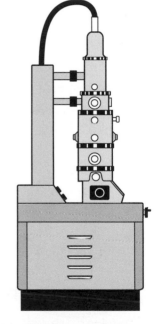

Electron microscope.

Look at the picture of the chloroplasts magnified 18,000 times using an electron microscope.

Then look at Topic 7A.3 to see what chloroplasts look like using a light microscope.

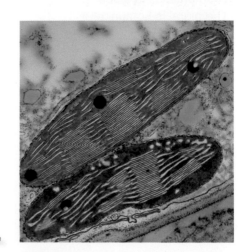

Chloroplasts.

Question 4

Changing ideas about babies

Ideas about where babies come from also changed with the invention of the microscope.

If you had lived more than 250 years ago, you probably didn't know exactly where babies came from. Look at the table

New evidence changed ideas about reproduction.

Evidence	Who and when	Fluid passed from a man into a woman to make a baby contains …
A fluid (semen) was involved.	Hippocrates (about 2500 years ago)	… tiny body parts.
Under a microscope, they could see tiny swimming things in semen.	Antonie van Leeuwenhoek, Nicolas Hartsoeker and others (over 300 years ago)	… 'animalcules'. Some scientists claimed to see miniature humans inside the animalcules from humans. They called them homunculi, the Latin word for 'little men'.
Experiments showed that both sperm and egg cell were needed to make a baby.	Lazzaro Spallanzani (about 200 years ago)	… sperm that joined with a woman's egg cell.

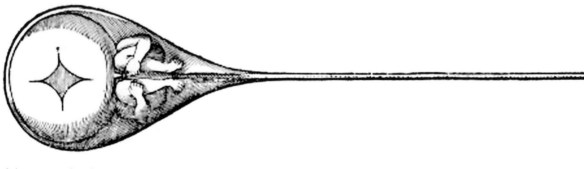

A homunculus in a sperm.
(The plural is homunculi.)

Question 5 ⟩ 6

7A.1

1 Name <u>two</u> organs that you can see on Aristotle's drawing.

2 Write down the names of <u>two</u> organs that you can see on the head scan.

3 Look at the picture of a thigh bone.
Name <u>three</u> tissues in this bone.

4 What do we use to see what the cells in these tissues are like?

7A.2

1 Who named cells?

2 Which part of the cell did Robert Brown name?

3 What do we call the theory that all plants and animals are made of cells?

4 Why did Robert Hooke draw the flea larger than life?

5 It would be useful to have a scale marked on the drawing of the flea. Explain why.

6 **a** How long is the ladybird in Leon's drawing?

   b A real ladybird is about 4 mm long. How many times longer is the ladybird in Leon's drawing?

7 Draw a ladybird magnified 20 times.
Remember to put a scale on your drawing.

8 Write down <u>two</u> jobs in which people draw things to scale.

7A.3

1   Look at the microscope views of living and non-living things.
Which ones do you think are of living things?
Explain your answers.

2   Write down <u>two</u> differences between plant and animal cells.

3   Which part controls what happens in a cell?

4   Cell membranes are very thin. Explain why.

5   Write down <u>three</u> parts that are in plant cells but not in animal cells.

6   Cells in plant roots are not green.
Suggest which parts are missing from root cells.

7A.4

1   Special cells line your breathing tubes.
What is the job of these cells?

2   How long is the nerve cell from your fingertip to your spinal cord?
(Hint: measure the distance from your backbone to your fingertip.)

3   Red blood cells don't have a nucleus.
Suggest how this helps them to carry more oxygen.

4   Root cell B in the picture takes in less water than root cell A.
Explain why.

5   A plant leaf is an organ. It is made of several different tissues.
What job does a leaf do?

6   There is more than one of some rooms in a house.
Write down <u>one</u> example.

7   There is more than one of some organs in your body.
Write down <u>one</u> example.

7A.5

1 300 years ago, it was easy for people to believe that living things sometimes appeared out of nowhere.
Write down <u>two</u> reasons for this.

2 Make a copy of the cell cycle diagram.
Complete the labels on your copy.
The missing words are <u>divides</u> and <u>grows</u>.
You will need to use one of the words twice.

3 Specialised cells can't divide. Suggest why not.

4 Before it divides, a nucleus makes a copy of the information it holds.
Suggest why

7A.HSW

1 What invention was needed before anyone was able to see cells?

2 Copy and complete the sentence.

In developing his microscopes, Abbe did experiments on _____ and _____.

3 Abbe worked in a scientific way.
In your group, discuss what that means.

4 Find out some examples of the magnifications obtained using electron microscopes.

5 Some scientists claimed to see 'homunculi' in sperm. Perhaps they saw what they wanted to see or didn't want to admit that they couldn't see anything.

   a Discuss in your group why the idea of 'homunculi' lasted for over 100 years.

   b Discuss in your group what can you learn from this story when <u>you</u> observe in science.

6 Who found the evidence that a sperm and an egg cell join to make the cell that grows into a baby?

You should already know   Outcomes   Keywords

Plants and animals produce young so that their kind survives.

In one kind of **reproduction**, a new life starts when the nuclei sex cells of a male and a female join. We call this kind of reproduction <u>sexual reproduction</u>.

Sex cells and fertilisation in plants

Flowers are the reproductive systems of plants.

Flowers produce special sex cells:

- pollen contains the male sex cell;
- ovules contain female sex cells.

Most pollen is carried from one flower to another by the wind or insects.

Question 1 2 3

When a pollen grain lands on a stigma:

- the pollen grain grows a tube down to the ovule;
- the nucleus of the male sex cell travels down this tube;
- this nucleus joins with the nucleus of the female sex cell in the ovule.

We call the joining of the nuclei **fertilisation**.

The cell that forms in fertilisation is the first cell of the new plant.

This cell then grows and divides to make a seed.

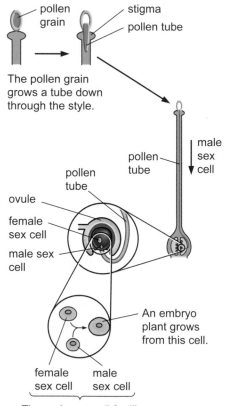

Pollen travels from the anther to the stigma of a flower of the same species. This is called **pollination**.

Pollen tube growth and fertilisation.

Question 4 5

Comparing fertilisation in plants and animals

In plants

A pollen grain has a tough outer wall. A tube grows:

- out of the grain;
- into the stigma;
- through the style;
- to the ovule.

The male sex cell travels down this tube to reach the ovule.

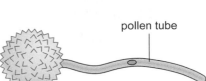

pollen grain

pollen tube

Pollen grain growing a pollen tube.

Question 6

In animals

The male sex cell is always inside the body or in water so it doesn't dry up.

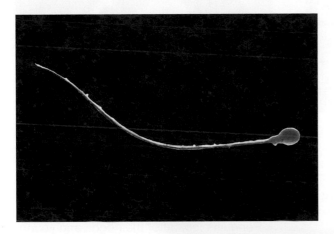

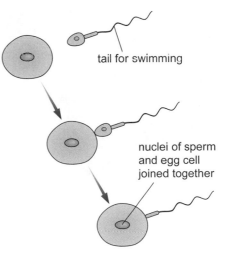

tail for swimming

nuclei of sperm and egg cell joined together

A male sex cell. We call it a sperm. A sperm swims to reach an egg.

A new life starts when the nucleus of a sperm joins with the nucleus of an egg cell. We say that the nuclei fuse. This fusing is called fertilisation.

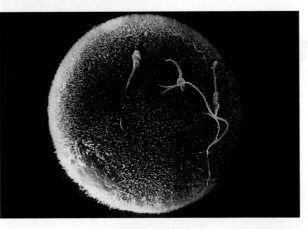

This female sex cell, or egg cell, is much bigger than the sperm cells around it.

Question 7 **8**

Patterns of reproduction in animals

Different ways	Description	Examples
external fertilisation	happens outside the body	fish, frogs
internal fertilisation	happens inside the body	birds, mammals

Different animals fertilise their eggs in different ways.

The eggs of fish and frogs don't have shells. They would dry up if they were laid on land. Each egg contains only a little stored food.

Most fish and frogs don't look after their eggs and young. They need to lay lots of eggs to make sure that a few survive.

Question 9 10 11

Penguins are birds. They lay one or two eggs. Each egg contains lots of stored food.

Penguins look after their eggs and young.

Mammals are different again. Their young grow in an organ inside the mother's body. We call this organ the uterus. After they are born, one or both parents feed and protect their young.

Cats look after their young until they are old enough to find their own food and protect themselves.

Question 12 13

Humans are mammals. So:

- human eggs have no shell;
- fertilisation happens inside the mother's body;
- the young develop in the mother's uterus;
- after they are born, the young feed on milk;
- one or both parents look after the young.

Often, other adults and older children help too.

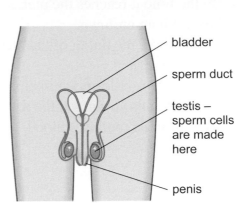

Male organs.

Question 1

A woman releases an egg cell from one of her ovaries about once a month. This is called **ovulation**.

An egg cell is fertilised when:

- sperm meets an egg cell in an oviduct;
- the nucleus of one of the sperm joins with the nucleus of the egg cell.

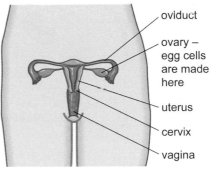

Female organs.

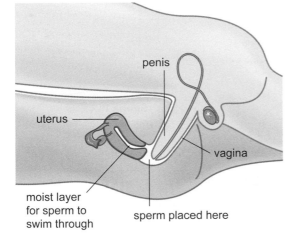

Over 200 million sperm cells travel from the testes through the penis and into the vagina.

The sperm and egg cells are really much smaller than this diagram shows. An egg cell is the size of a tiny speck of sand. You need a microscope to see sperm.

Question 2 **3** **4**

From fertilised egg to baby

- An egg cell is fertilised.
- It grows and divides as it travels down the oviduct into the uterus.
- It forms two cells, then four cells, then eight cells.
- By the time it reaches the uterus, it is a whole ball of cells. We call it an **embryo**.
- At this time, the lining of the uterus is thick. It has lots of blood vessels.
- The embryo settles into this lining. This is called **implantation**.
- Now the embryo can get the food and oxygen that it needs to grow from its mother's blood.

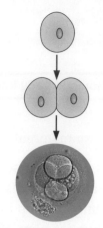

Cells split over and over again.

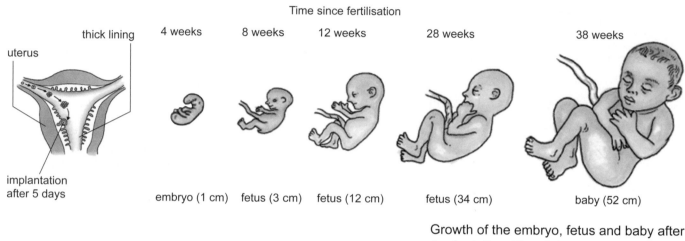

Growth of the embryo, fetus and baby after implantation. The pictures are not to scale.

Question 5   6   7 ─────────

Why children are like their parents

A fertilised egg cell contains the information for a new life. Part of this information comes from the mother's egg cell and part from the father's sperm. So parents, a child and its brothers and sisters are alike in many ways.

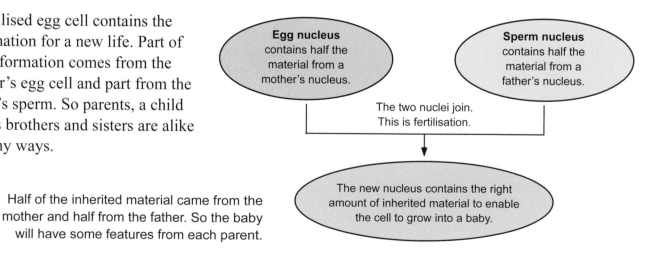

Egg nucleus contains half the material from a mother's nucleus.

Sperm nucleus contains half the material from a father's nucleus.

The two nuclei join. This is fertilisation.

The new nucleus contains the right amount of inherited material to enable the cell to grow into a baby.

Half of the inherited material came from the mother and half from the father. So the baby will have some features from each parent.

Question 8 ─────────

Some brothers and sisters are more alike than others.

Twins are born at the same time.

Non-identical twins:

- grow when two egg cells are fertilised by two different sperm;
- **inherit** from their parents
  - some features that are the same
  - some features that are different.

Identical twins:

- grow when one fertilised egg cell divides to form two separate embryos;
- inherit the same pattern from their parents.

Non-identical twins.

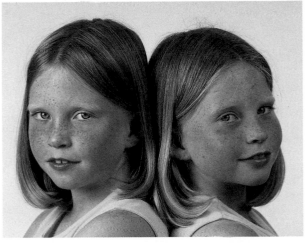

Identical twins.

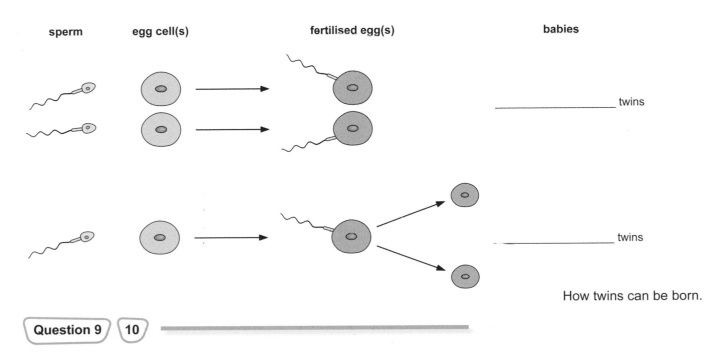

How twins can be born.

Question 9   10

7B.3 The menstrual cycle

You should already know

Outcomes

Keywords

To survive and grow, an embryo has to be implanted in the lining of the uterus. For this to happen, the uterus lining must be ready for it.

So there is a monthly cycle that links the release of an ovum (egg cell) to the growth of the uterus lining. This cycle is called the **menstrual cycle**.

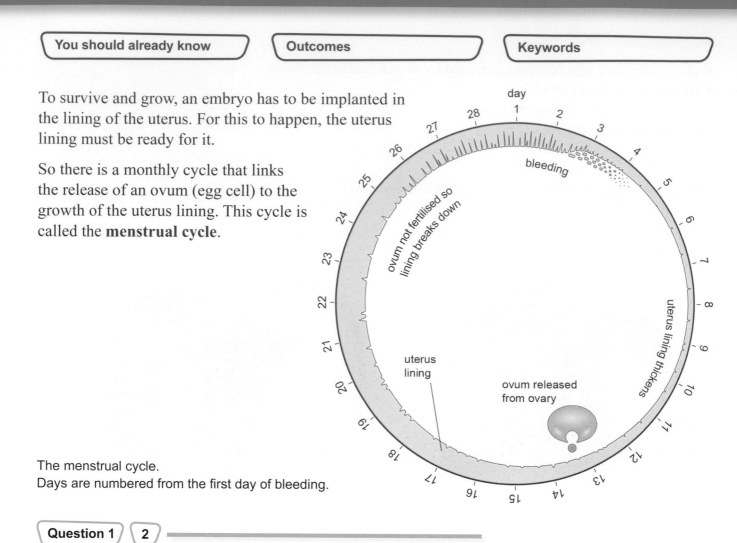

The menstrual cycle.
Days are numbered from the first day of bleeding.

Question 1 2

Special chemicals called **hormones** control the menstrual cycle. These hormones also change how a woman feels at different times in the cycle.

If an egg is not fertilised:

- the lining of the uterus breaks down;
- the woman 'bleeds', or has a 'period' – we call this bleeding **menstruation**.

If an egg is fertilised and an embryo is implanted:

- the lining does not break down;
- menstruation stops.

Question 3 4 5

You should already know | Outcomes | Keywords

As the **fetus** grows:

- the mother's body keeps the fetus at a constant temperature;
- the thick muscular wall of the uterus stretches;
- the **placenta** grows in the lining.

In the placenta, the blood of the fetus and the blood of the mother are very close but they do not mix. Substances pass across the placenta.

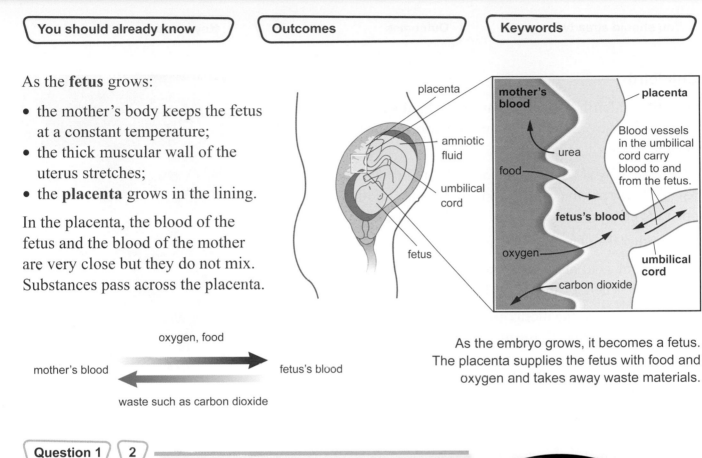

oxygen, food

mother's blood → fetus's blood

waste such as carbon dioxide

As the embryo grows, it becomes a fetus. The placenta supplies the fetus with food and oxygen and takes away waste materials.

Question 1 | 2

Sadly, harmful substances can also pass into the fetus's blood.

- On average, babies born to mothers who smoke weigh less and have more health problems than babies born to non-smokers.
- A few babies are born addicted to alcohol or other drugs.
- German measles virus can lead to a baby being born deaf and blind.

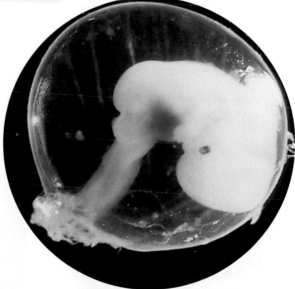

There is a bag of thin skin around the embryo. This bag is full of a liquid called **amniotic fluid**. This fluid supports the embryo and protects it against shocks.

Question 3 | Check your progress

You should already know   Outcomes   Keywords

Childbirth

We call childbirth 'labour' because it is hard work. The mother has to push the baby out of the uterus and through the vagina into the outside world.

When the baby is ready to be born, the mother starts to feel 'labour pains'. These are the contractions of the muscles of the uterus that open the cervix. Then the baby's head can go down into the vagina.

The mother then has to push hard to get the baby out.

The next job is to make sure that there is no fluid in the baby's nose and mouth. Then it can take its first breath.

A short time later, the uterus contracts again. It pushes the placenta out. We call this the <u>afterbirth</u>.

Question 1   2   3

The **umbilical cord** is clamped before it is cut.

The newborn baby is

- cleaned
- checked to make sure that there are no problems
- wrapped up to keep it warm.

Baby care

Looking after a baby is also hard work. Human babies are entirely dependent on other people.

Babies need protection against disease, accidents and animals.

Babies need to be kept clean.

The natural food for young mammals is milk from the **mammary glands**. A mother's own milk contains substances that destroy some of the micro-organisms that cause infections. That is one reason why many human mothers prefer to breastfeed their babies. As well as feeding the baby, it helps to protect it against infections.

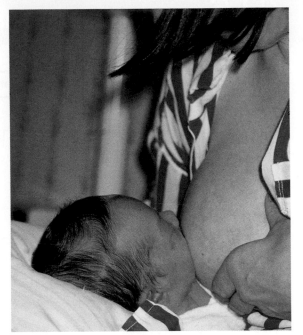

Babies need food and warmth.

Question 4

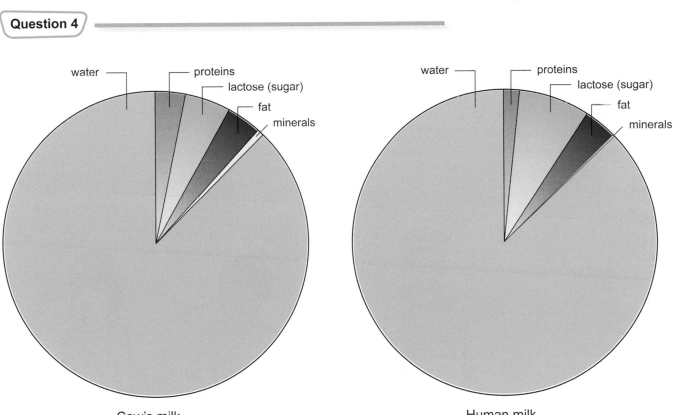

Cow's milk.

Human milk.

Human children depend on adults for many years. Babies have to learn to control their bodies, to talk and to walk. Usually many adults and older children help to care for them and to teach them. Children also learn many things for themselves.

Question 5 **6** **7**

| You should already know | Outcomes | Keywords |

Some children grow up faster than others. But all children grow faster at certain times. Children also change as they grow.

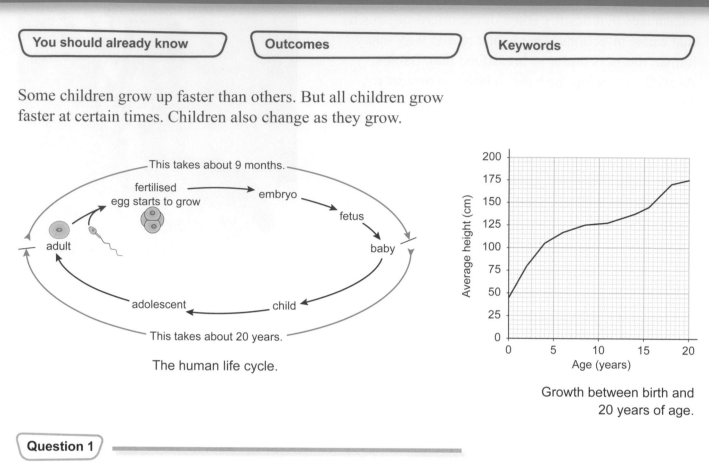

The human life cycle.

Growth between birth and 20 years of age.

Question 1

Sometimes it is difficult to tell whether a young child is a boy or a girl.

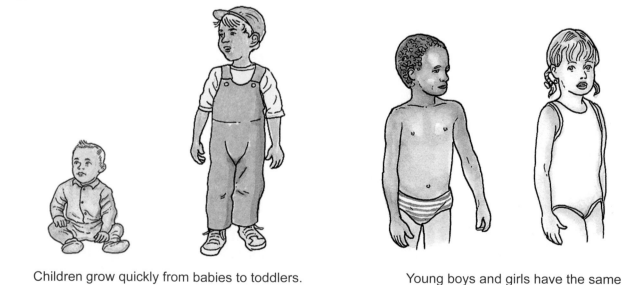

Children grow quickly from babies to toddlers.

Young boys and girls have the same body shape.

Question 2

One time of rapid growth and change is in the early teens.
This growth spurt starts at anything between 9 and 16 years old.
Often, it starts earlier in girls than in boys.

We call the time between childhood and adulthood **adolescence**.
At this time, a gland in the brain starts to make extra **hormones**.

These hormones

- make cells grow and divide faster
- make the testes and ovaries mature and produce sex hormones.

At **puberty**, the mature testes and ovaries start to release sex cells.

Women develop broader hips and
breasts as they grow up.

Question 3

The testes and ovaries make different hormones. So boys and girls
develop in different ways.

Body parts other than the sex organs develop special features.
We call these features **secondary sexual characteristics**.

Girls	Boys
pubic and underarm hair grow	pubic and underarm hair grow
breasts grow	facial and body hair grow
ovaries start to release eggs	voice deepens
monthly periods (of bleeding) begin	testes start to make sperm

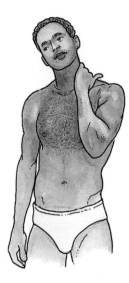

Usually, men have broader chests
and shoulders, and more muscle
than women.

Question 4   **5**

Sex hormones also cause emotional changes and affect behaviour.

So adolescence is often a difficult time, especially as changes take
place at different rates in different young people.

Question 6

Review your work

Summary ➡

You should already know

Outcomes

Keywords

Having a baby is sometimes a problem

So far in this unit, we have looked only at

- how humans make embryos
- how babies then develop.

But some couples need extra help to make a baby.

This may be because

- the woman doesn't release egg cells
- the man doesn't make sperm or makes faulty sperm
- the woman's egg tubes are blocked, which is sometimes the result of having a sexually transmitted disease.

Information

Bacteria and viruses cause several different **sexually transmitted diseases** (STDs).

An infected person passes them on during sex.

People can reduce the risk by using condoms.

It is important to treat STDs quickly.

Question 1   2 _____

Helping people to reproduce

- Doctors investigate whether the couple is producing sperm and egg cells and whether the woman's egg tubes are blocked;
- They can try **IVF** (**in vitro** fertilisation) using
  - the couple's own egg cells and sperm
  - sperm or egg cells from donors.

But the embryos don't always grow.

Question 3   4 _____

In IVF, egg cells are fertilised in a dish and then placed in the woman's womb.

Doctors used to implant three or four embryos. But this sometimes resulted in triplets or quads. These are more likely to be born too soon and to die. Now, doctors implant two embryos at the most.

This decision was based on evidence.

Question 5 _____

We can do it – but should we?

Scientists developed reproductive technologies such as IVF by applying what they knew about reproduction.

It has improved some people's lives. But some people think that it shouldn't be allowed. With developments such as IVF, we have to think about:

- whether or not to use them
- when and how to use them.

When you make decisions about issues such as the use of IVF, you are thinking about **ethics**.

To make a decision, you need

- to understand what can be done
- to think of the advantages and disadvantages of each alternative
- to decide what you think and to give your reasons.

These decisions are based on ethics and evidence.

Question 6

7B.1

1 Suggest <u>two</u> ways that pollen gets from one flower to another.

2 On which part of the plant does a pollen grain need to land for pollination?

3 Most pollen grains are wasted.
Suggest <u>two</u> reasons for this.

4 What is fertilisation?

5 What is a pollen tube for?

6 What stops the sex cells in pollen grains drying up?

7 In animals, what do we call:

  a the male sex cells?

  b the female sex cells?

8 A sperm is a specialised cell. What special feature helps it to reach the egg cell?

9 Shells protect the eggs of birds and reptiles.
Write down <u>two</u> things that shells protect eggs against.

10 A large female fish like a cod lays up to seven million eggs.
Suggest why she needs to lay so many.

11 Each cod egg contains only a little stored food. Why do you think this is?

12 In some animals, the eggs are fertilised inside the female. Why does this happen in:

  a birds?

  b mammals?

13 Eggs laid in water have less chance of surviving than a bird's eggs.
Suggest why.

7B.2

1 Write down the name of the organ that makes:

   a sperm;

   b egg cells.

2 In humans, does fertilisation happen in the oviduct, uterus (womb) or vagina?

3 Write down a list of the parts that a sperm cell passes through on its way from the testis to the egg cell.

4 How do the sperm get from the vagina into an oviduct?

5 How long does it take for the ball of cells to reach the uterus?

6 **a** What is implantation?

   b Why do fertilised egg cells have to become implanted in the lining of the uterus?

7 Before all its main organs have started to grow, we call the developing baby an embryo. Later, it looks like a baby but its organs are not fully developed. What do we call it then?

8 How much of the inherited material in the nucleus of a fertilised egg cell comes from the father?

9 Copy and complete the diagram that shows how twins are born.

10 Are non-identical twins more alike than any other brothers and sisters? Explain your answer.

7B.3

1 Why does the lining of the uterus thicken every month?

2 An ovum is released about half way through the cycle. Explain why this timing is important.

3 What do we call the time of the month when a woman is bleeding?

4 Where does the blood:

   a come from?

   b leave the woman's body?

5 Why does menstruation stop when a woman is pregnant?

7B.4

1 Look at the pictures. Write down the jobs of:
   a the umbilical cord;
   b the amniotic fluid.
2 Draw a diagram to show:
   a <u>two</u> substances passing across the placenta from the mother to the fetus;
   b <u>two</u> substances passing across the placenta from the fetus to the mother.
3 A pregnant woman has to take special care.
   Write down <u>three</u> things that she needs to avoid.
   Explain your answers.

7B.5

1 What do the muscles of the uterus do to push the baby out?
2 What is the afterbirth?
3 The umbilical cord is clamped before it is cut. Suggest why the cord is clamped.
4 Look at the pie charts. Write down <u>three</u> differences between human milk and cow's milk.
5 Milk is sometimes called a 'complete food'.
   But some things that humans need in their diet are not in milk.
   Write down one of them.
6 Not all mothers in the UK breastfeed their babies. In your group, discuss some advantages and problems of breastfeeding.
7 A newborn baby can't keep its body temperature constant.
   Suggest why not.

7B.6

1   On a copy of the human life cycle diagram, label:

    a   the time of birth;

    b   the <u>two</u> periods between birth and adulthood when a person grows fastest. Use the graph to help you.

2   Write down <u>two</u> differences between the baby and the toddler in the picture.

3   To your diagram for question 1, add:

    a   adolescence, the time between childhood and adulthood;

    b   puberty, the time when adolescents become sexually mature.

4   **a**   What are secondary sexual characteristics?

    b   Write down <u>two</u> examples of secondary sexual characteristics.

5   Look at the pictures and the table. Write down <u>two</u> changes that happen during adolescence to:

    a   both boys and girls;

    b   girls only;

    c   boys only.

6   There is no need to worry if you start the changes of adolescence earlier or later than your friends.
    In your group, discuss the reasons.

7B.HSW

1   Pupils are taught about the symptoms of sexually transmitted diseases in PSHE.
    In your group, discuss the reasons.

2   Treating sexually transmitted diseases as soon as possible is important. Discuss the reasons.

3   Often IVF doesn't work.
    Discuss how couples might cope with this.

4   The National Health Service limits the number of times that a couple can try IVF. Suggest why.

5   What is the evidence for implanting only one or two embryos?

6   Discuss the pros and cons of using IVF. (It's OK if your ideas are not the same as those of others in the class.)

7C.HSW Choosing a method for investigating animals

You should already know

Outcomes

Keywords

Some ways of investigating

There are different ways of doing investigations. You need to choose a way that will answer your question.

- You could observe or experiment in a laboratory investigation.
- You could use secondary sources such as books or the Internet. Information collected by other people is called **secondary data**.
- You could do field work. You can:
  - observe the behaviour of animals;
  - use sampling to do **surveys** of a habitat or of people.

> You have to use secondary sources to find out about the behaviour of large animals.
>
> You can use questionnaires to survey people.

Question 1 2

Investigations using living things

When you plan an investigation such as the one about the behaviour of woodlice on page 39, you need to think about:

- safety;
- the equipment you will use and how you will use it;
- how to make your test fair.

Sometimes you need to use apparatus, chemicals or living things that can be harmful. We call these things **hazards**.

You can look up hazards in books, or you can ask your teacher for help. To make sure that you and other people are safe, you need to ask yourself how high a **risk** there is of the hazard causing harm. We call this a **risk assessment**.

Then you decide if your investigation is safe to do. Sometimes the risk assessment helps you to see how to make the investigation safe, for example by wearing eye protection.

Question 3

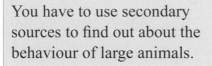

Enzymes in washing powder make my skin red and sore.

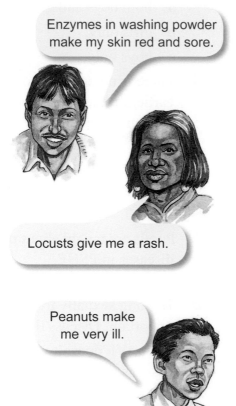

Locusts give me a rash.

Peanuts make me very ill.

Fair testing in an animal behaviour investigation

In an experiment, lots of things affect the results. We call these **variables**. We need to:

- vary the thing we are trying to find out about;
- control the other variables (this means keeping them the same).

Variables such as light and temperature are fairly easy to control.

But you need to gather data about a large **sample** of living things to allow for their variability.

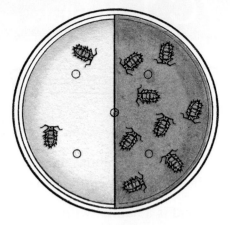

| Question 4 |

Woodlice vary. They might not all behave in the same way. So there are ten in this experiment and the experiment is repeated five times.

Investigating by observing

Some scientists find out about animal behaviour by watching them in the wild. For example, Karl von Frisch watched bees and their hives.

He found out that they were able to 'tell' each other where to collect nectar to make honey. The bees passed on information about both the direction and the distance to food using patterns of movements. He called the movements the 'waggle dance'.

| Question 5 |

Investigating animal behaviour using secondary sources

If you can't do your own investigations, you can use libraries and the Internet. You need to make sure that you can use:

- library catalogues;
- the index and contents page of a book;
- a search engine on the Internet.

The bee in the middle is dancing to tell the other bees where to find pollen. The dancing bee has just returned from a successful trip to find food. You can just see the full pollen sacs on its legs.

| Question 6 |

In the rest of this Unit, you will find examples of how to study living things and their habitats by observing and measuring in both field work and laboratory work.

| You should already know | Outcomes | Keywords |

Habitats are places where plants and animals live.

Your body is a habitat for micro-organisms and for parasites such as fleas, lice, flatworms and roundworms.

A pond is a habitat with:

- fresh (not salty) water;
- a small temperature range;
- less light as you go deeper;
- less oxygen as you go deeper;
- a range of food sources.

A plant or animal's habitat provides the right conditions for it to survive. Each plant or animal has features that suit it to the conditions. We say that the plant or animal is **adapted** to these **environmental conditions**.

Newt tadpoles spend all their time in the water. They have gills instead of lungs.

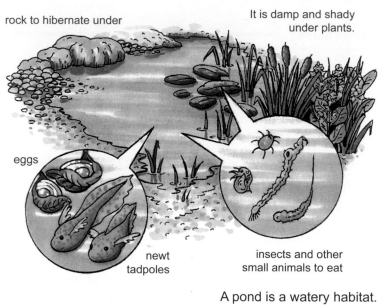

rock to hibernate under

It is damp and shady under plants.

eggs

newt tadpoles

insects and other small animals to eat

A pond is a watery habitat.

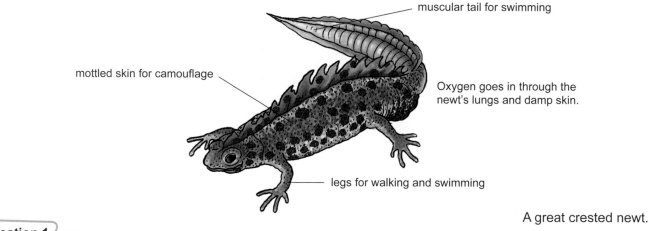

muscular tail for swimming

mottled skin for camouflage

Oxygen goes in through the newt's lungs and damp skin.

legs for walking and swimming

A great crested newt.

Question 1

Plants need light to make food. So water plant leaves need to be near or above the surface of the water.

Environmental conditions, such as the amount of light or water, are different in different habitats. So different habitats support different plants and animals.

Two land habitats.

Grassland	Woodland
plenty of light	trees shade the ground
fairly large range of temperatures	smaller range of temperatures
exposed to the wind	sheltered from the wind
fairly dry soil	damper soil
less humid air	more humid air

some animals shelter among plants, while others burrow in the soil	animals live in trees and other plants, in leaf litter and in burrows

Adaptations

Some adaptations for burrowing are:

- a cylindrical or streamlined shape;
- strong legs and clawed feet;
- good senses of
  - smell
  - vibration.

Burrowers often have a poor sense of sight.

A mole has strong claws for digging.

An earthworm has a long thin body and slimy skin.

A song thrush.

Question 2 3 4

| You should already know | Outcomes | Keywords |

Conditions such as light and temperature vary:

- from habitat to habitat;
- over a 24-hour period.

Marcus wanted to measure changes in temperature in the school greenhouse. He tried two different ways. He used a thermometer and a datalogger. (A datalogger collects and records information.)

The charts show Marcus's results.

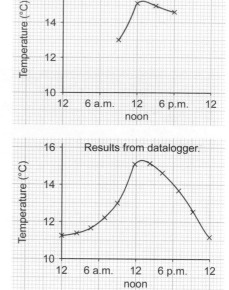

(Question 1) (2) (3)

Like you, other animals are adapted to daily changes.
Animals may be up and about only

- during the day
- when it is getting light or getting dark
- at night (we call these **nocturnal** animals).

The table shows animals seen or heard in a school garden at different times of the day.

Before school	During school	After school	Getting dark	After dark
squirrels	butterflies	butterflies	sparrows	bats
sparrows	bees	bees	midges	foxes
blackbirds	sparrows	squirrels	bats	owls
rabbits	kestrels	sparrows	foxes	moths
		kestrels	mice	earthworms

(Question 4) (5) (6)

Bats send out sounds and listen for echoes using their sensitive ears. Bats that feed on flying insects have small eyes. Bats that feed on nectar have large eyes.

Livingstone daises open only in the sunshine.

This bat feeds on the nectar of banana flowers, which are open at night.

Owls hear well and can see in dim light.

Investigating behaviour

Science isn't just about what other people have found out.

You can:

- ask questions;
- do **investigations** to find out the answers.

Question 7

For example, you might:

- want to find out about the behaviour of woodlice;
- suggest reasons why woodlice hide under stones;
- test one of your ideas using a choice chamber.

Question 8

You might say what you think will happen. We call that making a **prediction**. Like other scientists, you can <u>test</u> your prediction to see if you are right.

Suppose the woodlouse stops in the side that you predicted for a long time. You can't be sure that all woodlice would do the same because:

- there are many different kinds of woodlice;
- within each kind the woodlice vary.

In an investigation, you always have to think about:

- variation of the animals;
- which environmental conditions you will vary;
- which environmental conditions you will keep the same.

Question 9 **10**

Woodlice are born with this behaviour. We say it is **instinctive**.

Some behaviour is learned.
Scientists study it by doing experiments.

Other scientists are interested in how animals interact in families and other groups. They **observe** this social behaviour.

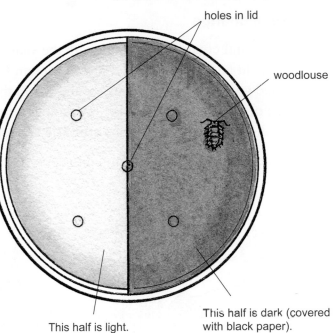

holes in lid

woodlouse

This half is light.

This half is dark (covered with black paper).

A woodlouse in a choice chamber.

Three different kinds of woodlouse.

Seasonal change

Environmental conditions change with the **seasons**. In the UK, the cold and frost of winter are a problem for many plants and animals. In some parts of the world the problem is shortage of water; in others it is high temperatures. We call these difficult conditions **climatic stresses**.

Plants and animals must be adapted to survive them.

spring

winter   summer

autumn

The seasons of the year.

There are fewer hours of daylight in winter.

> **Question 11**

Plants lose a lot of water from their leaves. In winter:

- it can be too cold to take any more water in;
- frost can damage some leaves, so many plants get rid of their leaves before the frosts start.

> A deciduous tree loses all its leaves at a particular season.
>
> An evergreen tree has leaves all the year round.

Pine needles are tough to withstand the cold. Their small surface area and waxy surface help to reduce water loss.

> **Question 12** **13**

Plants that lose their leaves can't make food in winter.
They are dormant. They use their stores of food to grow
new leaves in spring.

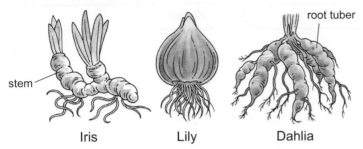

root tuber

stem

Iris   Lily   Dahlia

Some plants live through the winter as roots, stems or bulbs
under the ground. All the parts above the ground die.

Plants can also survive the winter as seeds.

Question 14 15 16

Problems for animals

The British winter brings problems for animals too. It's cold and
food is hard to find because there are fewer leaves and insects about.

Some birds fly south to warmer climates for winter.
We say that they **migrate**.

Other animals go into a deep sleep. They **hibernate**.

- Their temperatures drop.
- Their hearts and other organs slow right down.
- So they use stored fat very slowly.

Some butterflies hibernate.
Many survive the winter as pupae.
Adults come out of the pupae
in spring.

When it is winter in the
UK, it is warmer in Africa
and there are insects for
swallows to eat.

During hibernation,
hedgehogs use fat
stored in their bodies.

Question 17

Other animals stay active all the year round.

In autumn, these birds and mammals:

- store extra fat;
- grow a thicker coat of fur or feathers for insulation;
- may change colour for better **camouflage**.

Rabbits get fatter and
grow a thicker coat to
prepare for winter.

Question 18 19

Check your progress

7C.3 Feeding relationships

You should already know | Outcomes | Keywords

	Explanation	Example
Producers	make (produce) their own food	green plants
Consumers	eat (consume) plants and animals	humans
Herbivores	consumers that eat plants	rabbits
Carnivores	consumers that eat flesh	foxes
Predators	consumers that eat flesh; hunters	owls
Prey	food of predators	rabbits

Predators	Prey

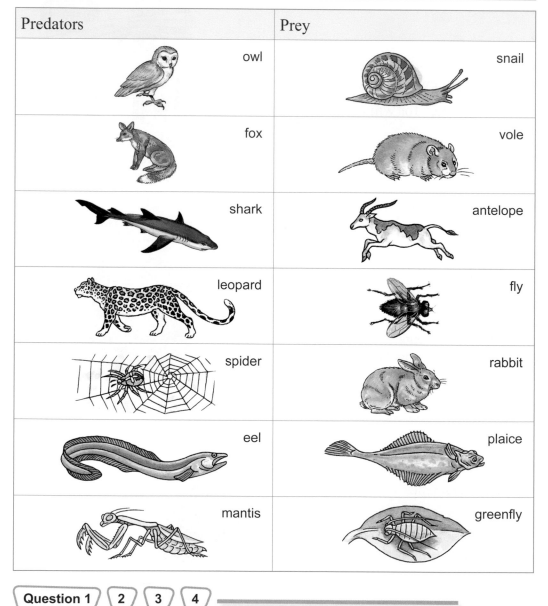

owl	snail
fox	vole
shark	antelope
leopard	fly
spider	rabbit
eel	plaice
mantis	greenfly

Question 1 2 3 4

Food chains

A **food chain** shows what eats what.

Only green plants make food so food chains begin with green plants. The arrows show the direction in which the food goes.

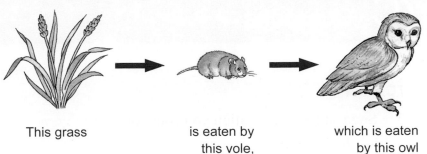

This grass   is eaten by this vole,   which is eaten by this owl

Question 5   6

The arrows also show the way that energy is transferred.

Green plants take energy from sunlight.

When an animal eats a plant, the energy is transferred to the animal.

Question 7

Food webs

Plants and animals belong to more than one food chain. So, we join food chains to make **food webs** for a habitat.

Part of a food web for a hedgerow.

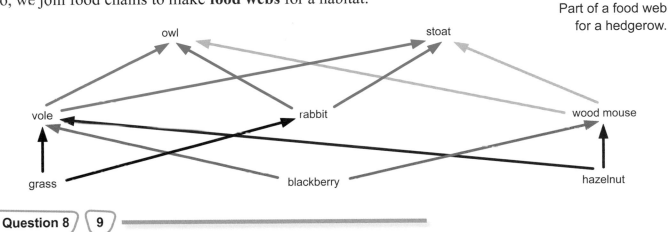

Question 8   9

A change in the number of plants and animals affects a food web.

If all the plants disappear, there is no food for the animals.

If all the owls die:

- the population of the animals that owls eat goes up;
- there will be more food for stoats so the number of stoats goes up;
- rabbits, voles and mice **compete** for food. If there are too many of them, some won't get enough to eat. Some will die. So there will be fewer of them.

Review your work

Question 10

Summary ➡

7C.HSW

1 Suggest an investigation you could do using

   a the Internet

   b a questionnaire.

2 Write down <u>three</u> possible hazards when you investigate
living things.

3 What is a risk assessment?

4 Suppose that you wanted to find out the average mass of the snails
in a garden.

   a How many snails would you sample?

   b How would you select your sample?

   Give reasons for your answers.

5 Use a library or the Internet to find out about one example of an
investigation into animal behaviour. Write down:

   a the name of the scientist;

   b the animal studied;

   c whether the investigation was by observation or experiment;

   d what he or she found out.

6 In this book:

   a use the contents page to find the page number for the start of
Unit 7B;

   b use the index to find the pages that mention food chains.

7C.1

1 Draw a large copy of <u>one</u> newt tadpole. Label the ways that the
tadpole is adapted to its habitat (to help you, look at the way the
adult newt is labelled).

2 List the adaptations for burrowing of:

   a the earthworm;

   b the mole.

continued

3 Suggest how each of these features helps rabbits to survive.
(These are <u>not</u> adaptations to burrowing.)

  a Their legs are longer than those of moles.

  b Their eyesight is good. They see well to both the front and the side.

4 Thrushes are birds that live in woodland.
Suggest why each of these adaptations of thrushes is useful.

  a They can fly.

  b They have good eyesight.

  c They see in colour.

  d They judge distance well.

  e They have speckled feathers that are good camouflage.

7C.2

  1 Describe the differences between the results shown on the two graphs.

  2 Which way of investigating temperature change do you think is best?
Write down <u>one</u> reason for your answer.
Note: when you answer this question, you are evaluating Marcus' methods.

  3 Marcus found problems with both methods. Suggest <u>two</u> possible problems of using:

  a a thermometer;

  b a datalogger.

  Note: when you answer this question, you are evaluating Marcus' methods.

  4 a When are foxes usually active?

  b When foxes are looking after cubs, they can be seen at any time. Why do you think this is?

  5 Why do you think the banana flower is light coloured, with scented nectar and open at night?

  6 Describe how these animals are adapted for hunting at night.

  a Bats.

  b Owls.

continued

7 Woodlice are mainly found under things such as big stones and dead leaves. There are many possible reasons for this. As a group, think of as many reasons as you can.

8 The woodlouse is walking around the choice chamber. Where do you think it will stop?
Explain your answer.

9 There are three kinds of woodlouse in the picture. Do you think that all three will behave in exactly the same way?
Explain your answer.

10 Write down some environmental conditions that you think affect woodlice.

11 The pictures show the same place in winter and summer. Write down <u>three</u> problems for plants and animals in winter.

12 Write down two advantages of having no leaves in winter.

13 The leaves of evergreens are adapted to surviving low temperatures and to keeping water in. Describe how.

14 Deciduous trees store food in their roots and stems. Why do they need to do this?

15 Only underground parts of some plants survive the winter.

   a Suggest why underground parts of plants are less likely to be killed than leaves.

   b Write down <u>one</u> plant that survives as an underground stem.

16 Seeds have adaptations that help them to survive.
Find out <u>one</u> example of an adaptation of a seed.

17 Swallows migrate between Africa and the UK. Write down <u>two</u> reasons for this.

18 Explain how rabbits are adapted to survive winter.

19 Animals store lots of fat in their bodies to prepare for winter.
Explain how this helps the survival of:

   a rabbits

   b swallows

   c hedgehogs.

7C.3

1   What is a predator?

2   Sort the predators in the table into groups of animals that:
- chase their prey;
- ambush their prey;
- build traps to catch their prey.

3   Write down <u>four</u> adaptations of predators.

4   Write down <u>four</u> adaptations of prey animals.

5   Food chains begin with green plants.
Explain this as fully as you can.

6   In the food chain, grass → vole → owl, name the plant, the predator and the prey.

7   **a**   Copy the diagram below. Next to it, draw a food chain, naming real plants and animals. Don't forget to include the arrows to show the direction the food and energy go.

Predator	Carnivore	Consumer
↑	↑	↑
Prey	Herbivore	Consumer
↑	↑	↑
Green plant	Green plant	Producer

   b   Notice that the herbivore and the carnivore are both called consumers. The energy passes to the herbivore first. So we call it the <u>primary consumer</u>. The carnivore is the second animal to get the energy. So we call it the <u>secondary consumer</u>. Add 'primary' and 'secondary' to your copy of the diagram.

8   **a**   Make a copy of the food web. Add your name to it. Then draw arrows to you from the things in it that you can eat.

   b   Draw a large arrow next to your copy of the food web to show the direction of energy transfer.

9   Food webs are better than food chains for showing what happens in a habitat. Explain why.

10 **a**   From the food web, write down <u>two</u> animals that compete to eat rabbits.

   b   Suppose all the rabbits catch a disease and die. Discuss in your group <u>two</u> effects that this would have on the food web.

7D.1 The same but different

A **species** is one kind of living thing.

Members of a species:

- have a lot of the same **characteristics**;
- are different from members of other species;
- produce fertile offspring only when they breed with each other.

Humans are all similar. They can reproduce and produce fertile offspring. So we say that they belong to the same species.

Humans all belong to the same species.

Question 1 | 2 | 3 —————

Variety is the spice of life!

There are differences between humans. We say that they **vary**.

We call the differences **variations**.

Some of the differences are hard to see.

All these girls have different blood groups.

Question 4 —————

Variations in other animals and plants

Humans vary. So do other animals. Dogs look different because they are different breeds. But they are all members of the same species.

basset hound

terrier

labrador

offspring 1

offspring 2

offspring 3

A family tree for a basset hound, a terrier, a labrador and their offspring.

pup 1

pup 2

Question 5 6

Plants from the same species also vary. Corn is one species of plant. Its fruits are called cobs.

We use different varieties for sweetcorn, animal food, popcorn, cornflour and cornflakes.

Corncobs come in different shapes, sizes and colours. We call these <u>varieties</u> of corn.

Question 7 8

You should already know

Outcomes

Keywords

Variations in a characteristic often run in families. We call them **inherited variations**.

Some characteristics are not inherited. They vary because of the environment in which a living thing develops.

Other variations have a mixture of inherited and environmental causes.

Variations that run in families

The Habsburg lip is a characteristic of the Habsburg family. This was one of the ruling families of Europe.

Emperor Maximillian (1459–1519).

Maximillian's grandson, Emperor Charles V (1500–1558).

Archduke Charles of Teschen (1771–1847).

Question 1 / 2

How we find patterns of inheritance

We can use a diagram called a **family tree** to show:

- how people are related to each other;
- characteristics that are passed on in a family;
- how a characteristic is inherited.

A characteristic is inherited when we see a strong pattern in a family tree.

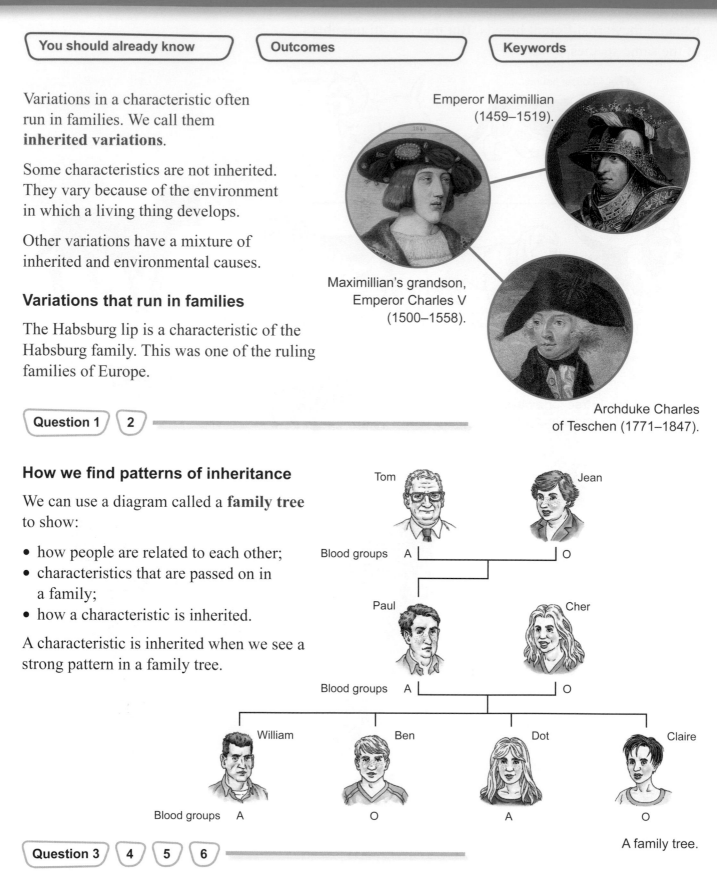

Tom Jean

Blood groups A O

Paul Cher

Blood groups A O

William Ben Dot Claire

Blood groups A O A O

A family tree.

Question 3 / 4 / 5 / 6

Environmental variations

Environmental variations are not inherited. They are a result of what happens to an animal or plant during its lifetime.

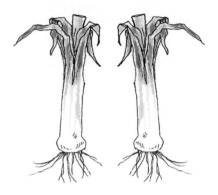

Leeks from the centre of the garden.

Leeks from the edge of the garden.

This is how leeks grow. These leeks are all the same variety.

Question 7 **8**

Joan and Ellen are identical twins. Ellen had a serious illness when she was nine, so she did not grow as tall as her sister.

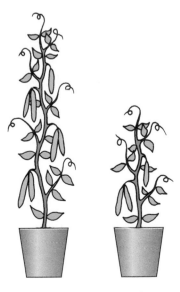

These pea plants grew in exactly the same environmental conditions.

Question 9 **10**

You should already know | Outcomes | Keywords

Members of the same species vary. But there is more variation between members of different species.

Gorillas are:

- similar to humans in some ways;
- different from humans in some key characteristics.

So gorillas belong to a different species.

Question 1

When you look for differences between animals, you have to look carefully. Careful observation is very important in science.

Books for identifying plants and animals use accurate drawings and descriptions to help us to tell one species from another.

Descriptions in stories and poems don't have to be so accurate. They are sometimes about only one characteristic.

Who is this...

...in the poem?

Question 2

Gorilla.

There once was a _____ called Nick
whose movements were sudden and quick.
He loved to pop out
and cause people to shout
but his wriggling legs made me sick!

Question 3

...in the scientific description?

Nick has eight legs.
He has two parts to his body, a head and an abdomen.
He has spinnerets that he uses to make silken threads.
He has hard outer parts called an exoskeleton to protect him.
Nick eats insects, so he is a carnivore.

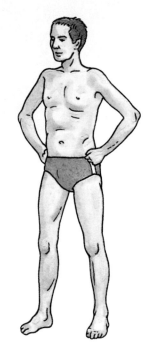

Human.

Question 4 **5** **6** **7**

Why details are important

Hoverflies and wasps look similar in many ways. But:

- wasps sting;
- hoverflies don't sting;
- hoverfly young eat the greenfly that damage plants.

So many people like to have hoverflies in their gardens, but not wasps.

Question 8 / **9** / **10** / **11**

Scientific description of hoverflies	Scientific description of common wasps
have a head, a thorax and an abdomen	have a head, a thorax and an abdomen
have six jointed legs	have six jointed legs
have bright black-and-yellow markings on their abdomens	have bright black-and-yellow markings on their abdomens
often feed on pollen and nectar from flowers	like sugary foods but mainly feed on meat
can hover	do not hover
have a margin on the edge of their wings	do not have a margin on the edge of their wings
have large, round compound eyes	have crescent-shaped compound eyes
do not have jaws	have jaws for biting
do not have a sting	have a sting

Hoverfly.

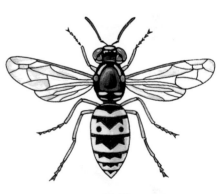

Common wasp.

Question 12

Centipede.

Millipede.

Check your progress

You should already know | Outcomes | Keywords

The police have files containing millions of fingerprints.
They use them to identify fingerprints found at crime scenes.

If they sort the fingerprints into groups with similar **characteristics**, they have to check only one group, not all of them.

Whorls | Loops | Arches

whorl

Question 1

There are lots of ways of sorting living things.

We often start by sorting them into green plants and animals.

living things
green plants   animals

Question 2

Then we sort these groups into smaller groups.
These pictures show one way of sorting animals into groups.

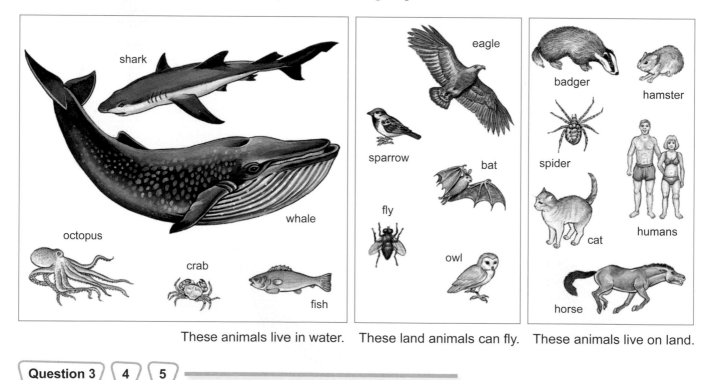

shark
octopus
crab
whale
fish

eagle
sparrow
bat
fly
owl

badger
hamster
spider
cat
humans
horse

These animals live in water.   These land animals can fly.   These animals live on land.

Question 3 / 4 / 5

An ancient way of sorting

Aristotle lived in Greece over 2000 years ago. He sorted plants and animals into groups. When he sorted them, he used sets of characteristics.

Before Aristotle, people grouped animals into land and water animals or winged and wingless animals.

Aristotle saw that some ants have wings and others don't. So he realised that a simple grouping using one characteristic doesn't work.

Aristotle (384–322 BC).

MAN
MAMMALS
WHALES
REPTILES + FISH
OCTOPUSES + SQUIDS
JOINTED SHELLFISH
INSECTS
MOLLUSCS
ZOOPHYTES   ASCIDIANS
JELLYFISH
HIGHER PLANTS   SPONGES
LOWER PLANTS
INANIMATE MATTER

Aristotle's sorting system.

Question 6

Sorting is useful

You know that **birds**

- have feathers
- have beaks
- have wings
- walk on two legs.

So if someone tells you that an eagle is a bird, you already know a lot of things about it.

You might see an animal that you haven't seen before but you recognise that it is a bird. So you look it up in a book about birds, rather than a book about all animals.

bat

eagle

dragonfly

Birds, bats and many insects fly. But bats and insects are very different from birds. So flying is not a useful characteristic for sorting animals.

Question 7

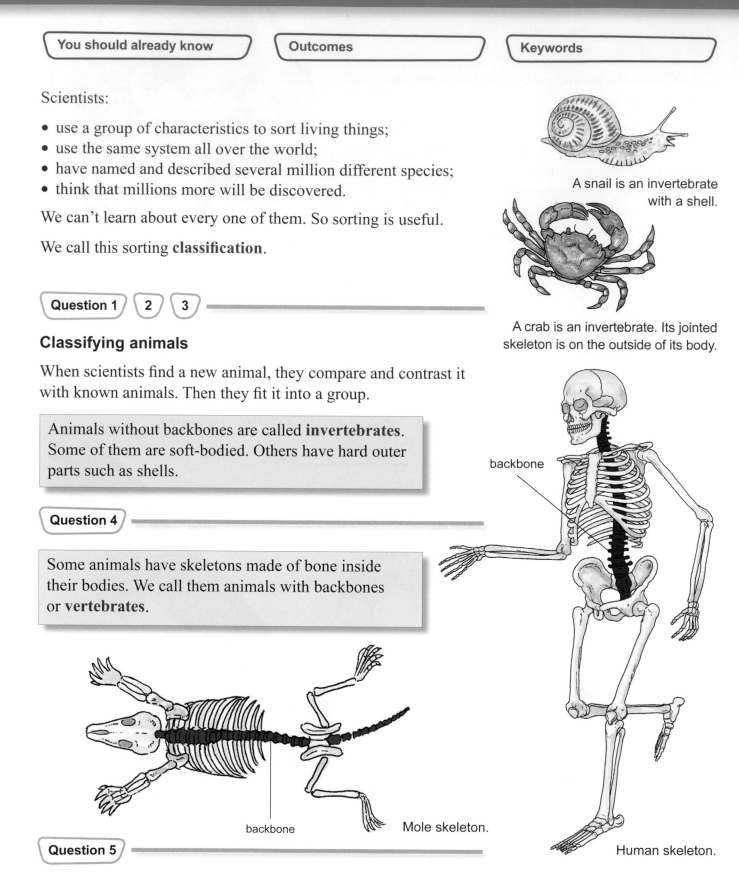

Scientists:

- use a group of characteristics to sort living things;
- use the same system all over the world;
- have named and described several million different species;
- think that millions more will be discovered.

We can't learn about every one of them. So sorting is useful.

We call this sorting **classification**.

A snail is an invertebrate with a shell.

A crab is an invertebrate. Its jointed skeleton is on the outside of its body.

Question 1 / 2 / 3

Classifying animals

When scientists find a new animal, they compare and contrast it with known animals. Then they fit it into a group.

Animals without backbones are called **invertebrates**. Some of them are soft-bodied. Others have hard outer parts such as shells.

Question 4

Some animals have skeletons made of bone inside their bodies. We call them animals with backbones or **vertebrates**.

backbone

backbone

Mole skeleton.

Human skeleton.

Question 5

Classifying vertebrates

We know of about 60 000 different species of vertebrates.
So we divide them into smaller groups.

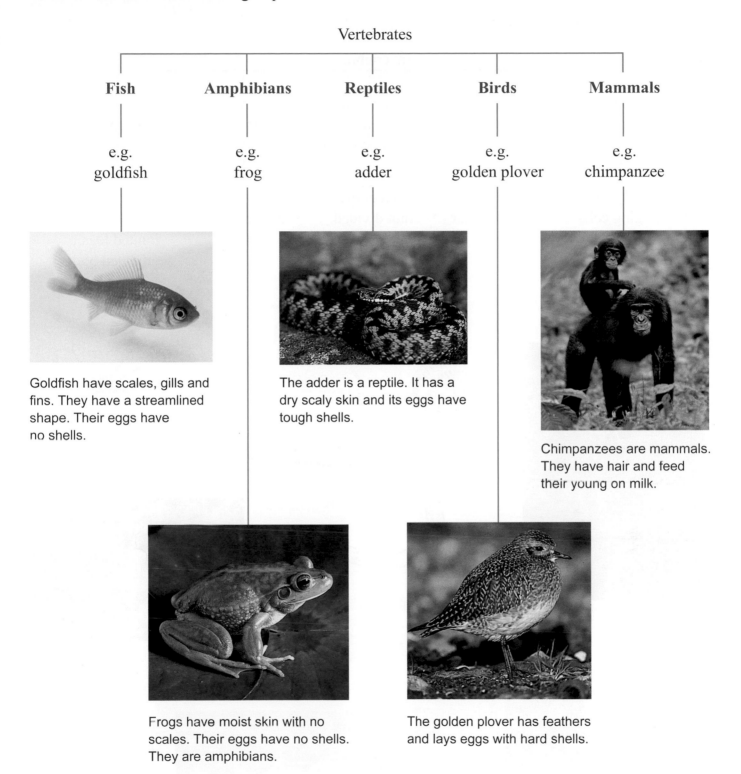

Vertebrates

Fish — **Amphibians** — **Reptiles** — **Birds** — **Mammals**

e.g.
goldfish

e.g.
frog

e.g.
adder

e.g.
golden plover

e.g.
chimpanzee

Goldfish have scales, gills and fins. They have a streamlined shape. Their eggs have no shells.

The adder is a reptile. It has a dry scaly skin and its eggs have tough shells.

Chimpanzees are mammals. They have hair and feed their young on milk.

Frogs have moist skin with no scales. Their eggs have no shells. They are amphibians.

The golden plover has feathers and lays eggs with hard shells.

Question 6 ⟩ 7 ⟩ 8 ⟩ 9

Invertebrates

Over nine-tenths of all species of animals are invertebrates.
They don't have bones.

We divide them into groups, too.

Invertebrates

Jellyfish e.g. sea anemone	Molluscs e.g. snail	Flatworms e.g. planarian and tapeworm	True worms e.g. earthworm	**Arthropods** e.g. spider
jelly-like body, stinging cells	shell, one muscular foot	flat body, not divided into segments	round body, divided into segments	hard parts on outside, jointed legs, segmented body

Question 10 ⟩ 11 ⟩ 12 ⟩ 13 ⟩

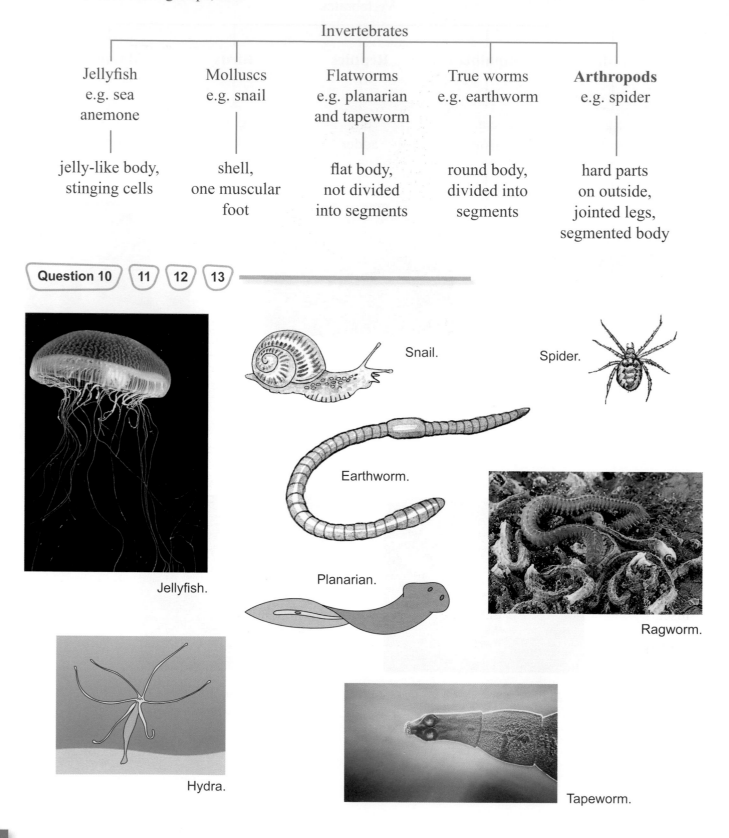

Snail.

Spider.

Earthworm.

Jellyfish.

Planarian.

Ragworm.

Hydra.

Tapeworm.

More groups

All the groups of invertebrates are very big. So we divide them into smaller groups.

More than three-quarters of all animal species are arthropods. We divide arthropods into four main groups.

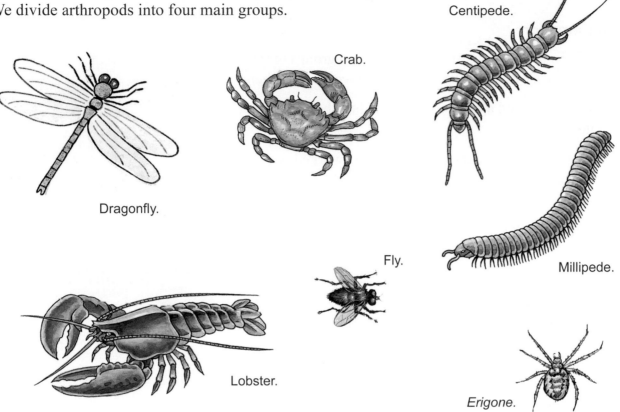

Centipede.

Crab.

Dragonfly.

Fly.

Millipede.

Lobster.

Erigone.

Question 14 **15**

Arthropod group	What do they look like?
crustaceans	two pairs of antennae; five or more pairs of legs
insects	three pairs of legs; one or two pairs of wings
spiders	four pairs of legs; no antennae
myriapods (many legs)	long body divided into segments; legs on every segment

Question 16

Review your work

Summary ➡

You should already know   Outcomes   Keywords

Sorting information

You learned in Topic 7D.4 that we sort things into groups to make the information easier to deal with. We say that we **classify** them.

Think about trying to find a book in a library if the books weren't classified into groups.

Over 2000 years ago in ancient Greece, Aristotle worked out a way of classifying living things. Look back at Aristotle's diagram in Topic 7D.4. Notice that we still use some of his groupings.

A Swedish scientist called Carl von Linne, also known as Linnaeus (1707–1778) worked out the main ideas of the modern **classification** system.

He started this work with his friend Peter Artedi (1705 1735). But Artedi died young so Linnaeus receives all the credit.

As well using the work of Aristotle, Ardeti and Linnaeus used ideas from

- Andrea Cesalpino (1519–1603), Italian
- John Ray (1627–1705), English
- Joseph Pitton de Tournefort (1656–1708), French

This is just one example of scientists building on the work of others – both from the past and from other cultures.

Title page of Volume 1 of Linnaeus' *Systema Naturae*.

Question 1 **2**

Linnaeus' aim was to classify all **species**. At this time, explorers were bringing back plants and animals that were unknown in Europe.

Linnaeus wanted to create order out of the chaos of these collections by grouping together similar and related organisms into classes, orders, genera and species.

Scientists from all over the developed world were able to use his system.

Question 3

Defining a species

You know that a species is a group of living things that

- have similar characteristics
- can breed together and produce offspring that can also breed.

Recognising that two living things belong to the same species is not always easy. John Ray first defined a species.

The same but different (species)

Horses and donkeys are similar. They can breed to produce mules. But mules cannot breed. So horses and donkeys are different species.

Different but the same (species)

These dogs look very different. But they can interbreed. So they are the same species.

Naming species

Before Linnaeus, the naming of plants and animals was also muddled. The lengths of names varied and the same plant had a different name in different places.

Linnaeus worked out a system of using two names.

Look at the information in the box.

Question 4 / 5

Once a scientist has described and named a species, scientists around the world use the same Latin name.

Locally, the name of the species stays the same.

Even within one country, the name of a plant or animal may vary. The plant *Alliaria petiolata* has different names in different parts of the UK. In some places it is called garlic mustard and in others Jack-by-the-hedge. It has other names too.

Question 6 / 7

In Linnaeus' system, species have

- a generic name
  (of the **genus**)

- a specific name
  (of the species).

All humans alive now belong to the same species,
    Homo sapiens.
      /   \
  (genus)   (species)

7D.1

1 Why do we group all humans together as one species?

2 Write down <u>four</u> characteristics of all humans.

3 Write down <u>three</u> differences between the people in the photograph of people in the street.

4 Look at the pictures of girls.

  a Write down <u>one</u> difference that you can see.

  b Write down <u>one</u> difference that you cannot see.

5 Write down:

  a <u>four</u> characteristics of dogs;

  b how each of these characteristics varies.

6 The different dogs in the pictures belong to the same species. How do you know?

7 Write down <u>three</u> differences between the cobs in the pictures.

8 All the cobs belong to the same species. Explain how we could prove it.

7D.2

1 Look carefully at the Habsburg family pictures. Describe the Habsburg lip.

2 Discuss what information you need to decide whether the Habsburg lip is inherited or not.

3 Look at the family tree. How many generations does it show?

4 Write down <u>two</u> ways in which Paul is similar to his parents.

5 Write down <u>two</u> other characteristics that are inherited in this family.

6 For each statement, say whether it is TRUE or FALSE. In each case, write down <u>one</u> piece of evidence.

  a Boys always inherit characteristics only from their fathers.

  b Some characteristics seem to miss one generation.

  c Children are identical to their parents.

  d Children of the same family can be very different.

continued

7 The leeks in the picture show environmental variation.
    Suggest <u>three</u> differences in the environment that could have
    caused the variation.

8 The height of the pea plants in the pictures is an inherited variation.
    Explain how we know this.

9 Look at the picture of the identical twins.
    Write down <u>two</u> characteristics of Joan and Ellen caused only by:

   a inheritance;

   b the environment.

10 Human height is partly an inherited and partly an environmental
    variation. Use the information about Joan and Ellen to explain this.

7D.3

1 Look carefully at the pictures. Write down <u>three</u> differences
    between the human and the gorilla.

2 Read the poem. Write down <u>three</u> animals that the poem could
    be describing.

3 Now read the description of the same animal. What type of animal
    do you think it is now?

4 **a** Write down <u>one</u> piece of information about Nick's structure that
    is in the poem.

   b The description gives you more information about this part.
    Write down that extra information.

5 What does the poem tell you about Nick that is not in
    the description?

6 In the description, find words that match the definitions a to d.

   a An animal that eats other animals.

   b The tail end of the body.

   c A skeleton on the outside of a body.

   d Tiny finger-like body parts that make silken threads.

7 Write a short poem that includes some of the scientific words in
    the description.

8 It is useful to be able to tell the difference between a wasp and a
    hoverfly? Explain why.

9 Look at the table. Write down <u>three</u> characteristics that hoverflies
    and common wasps share.

continued

10 Write down <u>two</u> characteristics that help you to tell the difference between a hoverfly and a common wasp.

11 Details are important when we describe animals such as these insects. Explain why.

12 Look at the pictures of a centipede and a millipede. Use the words below to write a description of each one.
- **Jointed leg**: leg with more than one joint (or bend) along its length.
- **Segments**: sections along the body.
- **Antenna**: long, thin projection on the head.

7D.4

1 Which file do you think the police will check to identify the fingerprint in the picture?

2 Plant and animal cells are different.
What other differences help you to separate plants and animals into groups?

3 The way the animals on this page are sorted into groups is <u>not</u> very useful.
Explain why.

4 Write down <u>two</u> animals that are separated in these groups that you think should be in a group together.

5 Sort the animals in the pictures into <u>two</u> groups using a different characteristic.

6 Aristotle used sets of characteristics for his grouping system. Suggest why.

7 Write down <u>three</u> facts about an eagle.

7D.5

1 What do we call it when we sort things into groups?

2 Why do we sort living things into groups?

3 It is useful for all scientists to use the same classification system. Suggest why.

4 Describe the hard body parts of <u>two</u> invertebrates.

5 The skeletons of different vertebrates are alike in lots of ways.
Look at the skeletons of the human and the mole.
Write down <u>three</u> ways that they are similar.

6 Look carefully at the diagram and pictures on this page.
Write down <u>one</u> characteristic that all these animals share.

continued

7   Mammals are different from the other groups of vertebrates.
    Write down <u>two</u> differences.

8   Write down <u>two</u> differences between amphibians and reptiles.

9   Newts are amphibians.
    From this information only, write down <u>two</u> things that you know
    about newts.

10 Write down <u>one</u> characteristic that all invertebrates share.

11 Look carefully at the diagram. The planarian and the earthworm are in
    different groups.
    Write down <u>two</u> differences between them.

12 The hydra and the jellyfish belong to the same group of invertebrates.
    Write down <u>two</u> characteristics that they share.

13 The ragworm is in the same invertebrate group as the earthworm.
    Suggest why these animals are classified in the same group.

14 Look carefully at the pictures of arthropods. Write down <u>two</u>
    characteristics that all arthropods share.

15 What <u>two</u> characteristics could you use to split this big group?

16 Look carefully at the pictures and the table.

    a   Which invertebrate group does each of these animals belong to?
        dragonfly   centipede   crab   *Erigone*

    b   Explain why you chose the group you did for each animal.

7D.HSW

1   On whose work did Linnaeus build?

2   Look at the picture. *Systema Naturae* is written in Latin.
    Suggest why a Swedish scientist published his work in Latin.

3   Discuss why we classifying living things into big groups then into
    smaller and smaller groups.

4   The Latin name for garlic mustard is *Alliaria petiolata*.
    Write down

    a   the genus the it belongs to

    b   its specific name.

5   There are rules about how scientists write the Latin names.
    What is the same about the way the Latin names of humans and garlic
    mustard are written down?

6   Suggest why scientists use an agreed set of names for living things.

7   Look up garlic mustard on the Internet or in a book about flowering
    plants to find some other names for it.

7E.1 What acids and alkalis are like (HSW)

Acids are all around us

Many things around us contain **acids**.

Some acids are in the food we eat. They give food a sharp, sour taste.

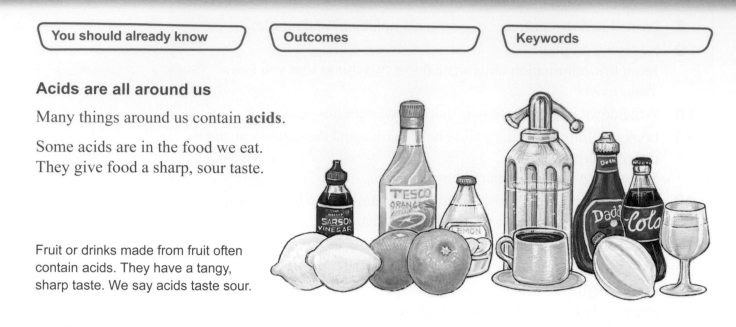

Fruit or drinks made from fruit often contain acids. They have a tangy, sharp taste. We say acids taste sour.

Question 1

In the 18th century, sailors could be at sea for a long time.

If they did not get fresh fruit often enough, they became ill with a disease called scurvy.

Scurvy is caused by a lack of vitamin C. It can be fatal.

Captain Cook discovered Australia. He made his sailors eat limes and lemons. This stopped them getting scurvy.

Lime juice prevents scurvy because it contains vitamin C.

Vitamin C is a **weak** acid so it tastes sour.

Lime juice tastes sour.

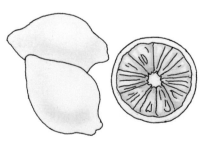

Limes and lemons taste sour because they contain citric acid. They prevent scurvy because they contain vitamin C. This is also an acid, but it is very weak.

Question 2

Some acids are dangerous

Some acids are **strong**. They are risky to use.

Hydrochloric acid has a **hazard** warning sign.

The sign tells you hydrochloric acid is **corrosive**. It will attack your skin and start eating it away.

This is the warning sign for corrosive.

CORROSIVE

Question 3

When you mix acid with water, we say that you **dilute** it. This makes the acid less dangerous.

If you spill an acid, you should wash the area with lots of water to dilute the acid.

Dilute acids are still harmful.

We use a black cross to warn people about them.

h

i

This is the sign for **harmful**.

This is the sign for **irritant**.

Question 4

About alkalis

The substances shown in the picture contain **alkalis**. Acids and alkalis can cancel each other out when they mix.

All these substances contain alkalis.

Strong alkalis like **sodium hydroxide** are just as dangerous as the strongest acids. They are also corrosive.

When you get alkali on your skin, it dissolves your skin away.

Your skin feels soapy. You get a chemical burn.

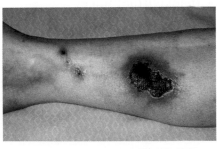

These burns were caused by an alkali called sodium hydroxide.

Question 5

You should already know

Outcomes

Keywords

Sodium hydroxide, hydrochloric acid, lemonade and water are all colourless liquids. They do different things when you add red cabbage juice to them.

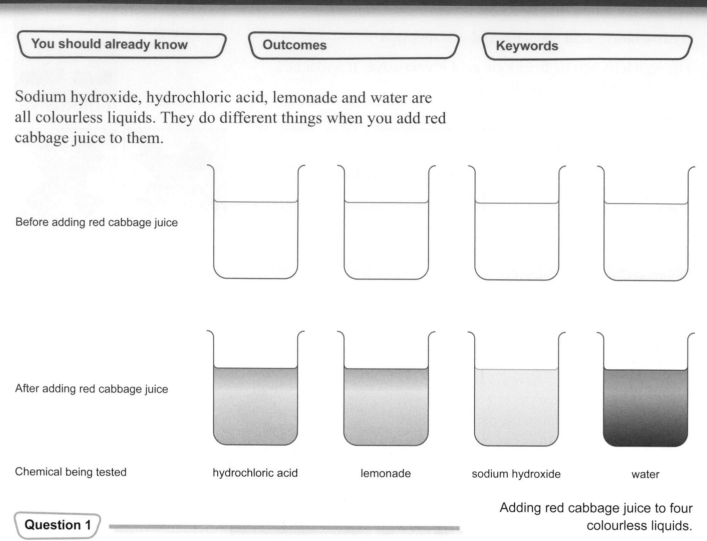

Before adding red cabbage juice

After adding red cabbage juice

| Chemical being tested | hydrochloric acid | lemonade | sodium hydroxide | water |

Adding red cabbage juice to four colourless liquids.

Question 1

The colours of red cabbage juice show whether a substance is an acid or an alkali.

We can use juices from other plants. For example we can use:

- beetroot juice;
- blackcurrant juice;
- a plant dye called litmus.

These substances are all **indicators**.

Indicators show a different colour in acid to the one they show in alkali.

Question 2

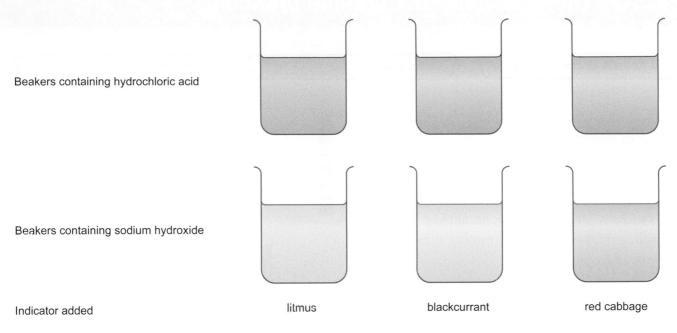

Beakers containing hydrochloric acid

Beakers containing sodium hydroxide

Indicator added   litmus   blackcurrant   red cabbage

The colours of three indicators in acid and in alkali.

Hydrochloric acid is a strong acid.

Sodium hydroxide is a strong alkali.

Question 3

Litmus is a dye. It is a very common indicator. It is purple when it is in a substance that is neither alkali nor acid. This type of substance is called a **neutral** substance.

Litmus turns red in acids. Litmus turns blue in alkalis.

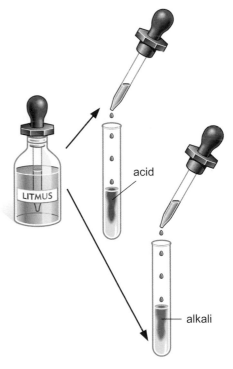

Substance	Litmus colour	Type of substance
sodium hydroxide	blue	alkali
vitamin C	red	acid
water	purple	neutral
calcium hydroxide	blue	alkali

Litmus turns purple in water. This shows us that water is neutral.

This means water is neither acid nor alkali.

Question 4 **5**

You should already know   Outcomes   Keywords

Litmus shows whether something is acidic, alkaline or neutral.

Universal indicator is a special type of indicator.

It tells us how <u>strong</u> or <u>weak</u> an acid or an alkali is. It is made by combining other indicators together.

When hydrochloric acid is concentrated, it is very acidic. It turns universal indicator red. Lemonade is a weak acid – it is a lot less acidic than concentrated hydrochloric acid. It turns universal indicator yellow.

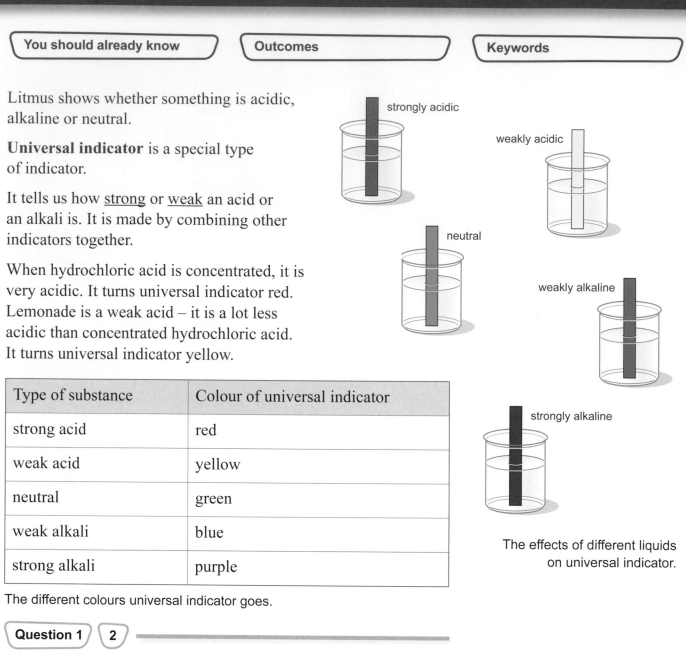

The effects of different liquids on universal indicator.

Type of substance	Colour of universal indicator
strong acid	red
weak acid	yellow
neutral	green
weak alkali	blue
strong alkali	purple

The different colours universal indicator goes.

Question 1 **2**

The strengths of acids and alkalis are measured on a scale called the **pH scale**.

The scale goes from 0 to 14.

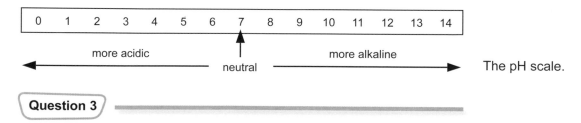

The pH scale.

Question 3

The different colours of universal indicator are matched to the numbers on the pH scale. When you buy universal indicator, you can buy a colour chart like this.

pH numbers

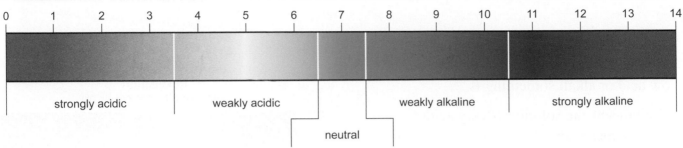

| 0 | 1 | 2 | 3 | 4 | 5 | 6 | 7 | 8 | 9 | 10 | 11 | 12 | 13 | 14 |

strongly acidic   weakly acidic   weakly alkaline   strongly alkaline

neutral

Strong acids are between 0 and 3 on the scale. Concentrated hydrochloric acid has a pH of 1.

The numbers 4 to 6 tell us the liquid is a weak acid. Lemon juice is a weak acid. Its pH is 5.

Number 7 tells us the liquid is neutral. Water has a pH of 7. It is neither acid nor alkali. It makes universal indicator green.

Numbers from 8 to 14 are for alkalis. Sodium hydroxide is a strong alkali.

This chart shows what happens when you test some different substances with universal indicator.

A colour chart for universal indicator that shows the pH scale.

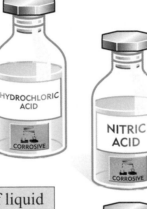

Liquid	Colour of universal indicator	pH	Type of liquid
nitric acid	red	1	strong acid
vinegar	yellow	5	weak acid
ammonia solution	purple	14	strong alkali
sodium bicarbonate solution	blue	9	weak alkali
salt water	green	7	neutral

Question 4 5 6

You should already know

Outcomes

Keywords

Adding acid to alkali

Remember, the colour of universal indicator tells us how acid or alkali something is.

- Red means the solution is very acidic.
- Purple means the solution is very alkaline.
- Green means the solution is neutral.

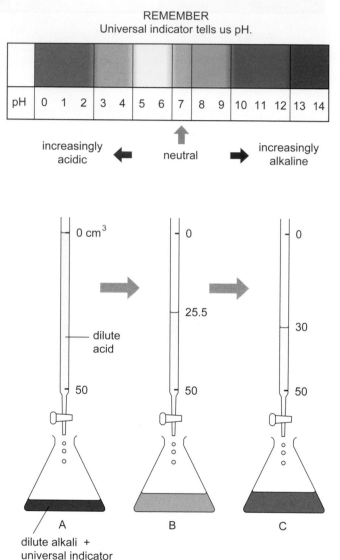

REMEMBER
Universal indicator tells us pH.

| pH | 0 | 1 | 2 | 3 | 4 | 5 | 6 | 7 | 8 | 9 | 10 | 11 | 12 | 13 | 14 |

increasingly acidic   neutral   increasingly alkaline

The diagrams show acid being dripped from a tube into a flask of alkali.

There is universal indicator in the alkali solution.

At the start the pH is high because the flask contains a lot of alkali. The pH is about 13 or 14.

After about half the acid has been added, the pH has dropped to about 7.

Flask B contains a neutral solution. The acid has cancelled the alkali out.

The acid and the alkali **react** to make a neutral solution.

If you keep adding acid, the pH keeps falling.

Eventually, if you add enough acid, you get an acidic solution with a pH of about 1.

This type of reaction is called **neutralisation**. You have to add just the right amount of acid to an alkali to cause neutralisation.

- Too much acid makes an acidic solution.
- Not enough acid leaves an alkali solution.

Question 1 2

A neutralisation experiment

The diagram shows an experiment with
hydrochloric acid, water and washing soda.

The washing soda crystal dissolves in the water
around it. You add a few drops of universal
indicator and leave it for a few days.

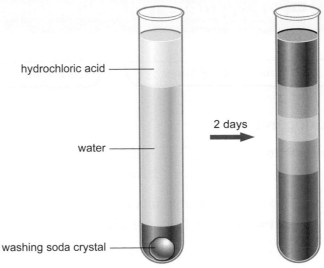

Question 3 4

The photograph shows the experiment with hydrochloric acid,
washing soda and water after a few days.

- The hydrochloric acid has turned the universal indicator red at
  the top of the tube.
- The washing soda crystal has dissolved in the water near it.
- The universal indicator is blue around the washing soda.
- This means the washing soda solution is alkaline.
- The washing soda gradually moves up the test tube.
- The hydrochloric acid gradually moves down the test tube.
- The washing soda neutralises the hydrochloric acid where
  they meet.

Neutralisation happens where the colour is green, just under the
yellow section.

Question 5 6

The experiment after a few days.

Check your progress

| You should already know | Outcomes | Keywords |

Curing indigestion

Indigestion is caused by too much acid in the stomach. You can take medicine for this.

Indigestion medicine contains an alkali. The alkali neutralises the stomach acid.

It is important that the alkali in the medicine is weak. If it is too strong, it will corrode your insides.

Some indigestion cures contain carbonates.

When these neutralise the acid in your stomach, they make **carbon dioxide** gas.

Unfortunately the gas produced can make you burp!

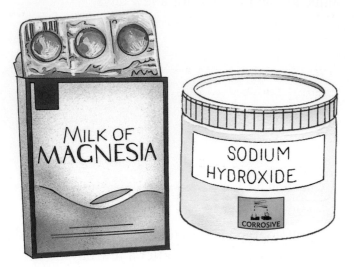

One of these is a medicine for indigestion.

Question 1 **2**

Here are the results of some tests with indigestion tablets.

Tablet	Cost per tablet	Amount of acid neutralised (cm³)	Amount of gas produced (cm³)	Time taken to neutralise the acid (minutes)
brand A	3p	25	none	3
brand B	4p	20	none	10
brand C	5p	30	15	2

Question 3

Toothpaste

Your mouth is full of bacteria.

Bacteria feed on bits of food left in your mouth.

When bacteria feed, they produce an acid. The acid attacks your teeth. It makes your teeth decay.

When you brush your teeth, you get rid of the bits of food and some of the bacteria.

Toothpaste is a weak alkali. The toothpaste neutralises the acid that the bacteria produce. This helps to protect your teeth.

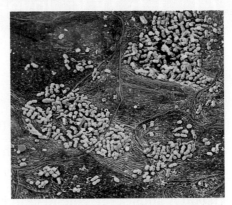

Bacteria on a human tongue.

Question 4

Making cakes rise

Baking powder is an ingredient in some cake recipes. It contains both an acid and an alkali.

When it is in the cake, the acid and alkali neutralise each other and produce carbon dioxide gas.

The carbon dioxide gas makes the bubbles in sponge cakes.

Question 5

The pH of this toothpaste is 8 because it contains sodium bicarbonate.

Acid rain

Pollution from factories and power stations produces acid gases in the air. Rainwater dissolves these acid gases and becomes acidic.

The water in rivers and lakes becomes slightly acidic.

In Scandinavian countries, they add crushed limestone to their lakes to neutralise the acidity caused by acid rain.

Some soil is more acidic than other soil. Serious gardeners test their soil using universal indicator so they know whether it is acid or alkali.

In some areas, the soil is too acidic for any plants to grow well.

Lime is the common name for one alkali.

Farmers spread lime on fields to neutralise some of the acid in the soil.

Adding lime reduces the acid in the soil and plants can now grow well.

Question 6

Review your work

Summary ➡

You should already know | Outcomes | Keywords

Investigating the effect of temperature on a reaction

Some pupils are investigating whether the temperature of hydrochloric acid affects its reaction with a metal.

Group A adds some zinc to cold hydrochloric acid and some iron to some hot hydrochloric acid. Both test tubes produce bubbles of hydrogen gas at the same rate.

Group B think group A's test is not fair because they have used different metals as well as acid that is at different temperatures.

This means that they cannot tell if it is the temperature or the metals having an effect.

Group B add zinc to both cold and hot acid, and repeat the experiment with iron. They notice that zinc gives off more bubbles than iron if the acid is at the same temperature.

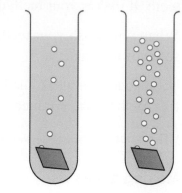

Zinc in cold acid and hot acid.

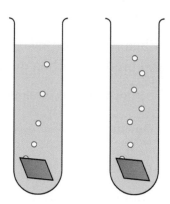

Iron in cold acid and hot acid.

Question 1 2

The teacher explains to group A that their method does not give reliable evidence. This is because they have changed more than one thing at once.

When you decide how reliable an experiment is it is called **evaluation**.

Deciding what to do to make your method of working safe is called a **risk assessment**. Look at the pupils in the diagram.

- The bottles of acid are too close to the back edge of the desk.
- One pupil has a test tube very close to his body.
- Their lab coats are open and not protecting the front of their bodies.
- The pupils are not aware of what the other is doing.

Part of a risk assessment is to state what you would do to reduce the risk.

Question 3

Safety in science

When scientists plan investigations they need to think about

- the plan of what to do
- how to make any tests fair
- the equipment and substances they use
- safety.

You can look up **hazards** for different substances in books or on cards that are published about the substances. Some substances have hazard warning signs on their containers.

In a risk assessment, you identify each hazard and decide what to do to reduce it.

This is the warning sign for corrosive.

CORROSIVE

This is the sign for **harmful**.

This is the sign for **irritant**.

Hazardous chemicals have warning labels. You need to be able to recognise them.

A funnel is used to fill a tube with hydrochloric acid.

A tube is used to put a measured amount of sodium hydroxide into a flask.

Some indicator is added to the flask.

The photographs show part of an experiment in which hydrochloric acid is added to sodium hydroxide. There are several safety features.

- The person is wearing goggles.
- The person is standing up.
- A funnel is used to direct the acid into a narrow tube.
- The substances used are clearly labelled.

Risk assessment is one part of science that affects the way people think and behave.

Standing up is the result of a simple risk assessment. You can reduce the risk of spilling harmful chemicals on your legs if you stand up. If there is a spill on the worktop, it will drip onto the floor and not onto your lap.

Question 4 **5**

Even when you have done a risk assessment, accidents can happen. This might be because your risk assessment was not good enough. It might be because you are not following your risk assessment. It might just be due to some unexpected event, a pure accident.

Question 6 **7**

Someone distracted this student during an experiment and she has spilled alkali onto her hand.

7E Questions

7E.1

1 Look at the picture. Give an example of something that contains an acid.

2 What word best describes the acid taste of lime juice?

3 What does the word 'corrosive' mean?

4 What substance do you mix with an acid to dilute it?

5 What can an alkali cause on your skin?

7E.2

1 What colour does red cabbage juice turn when added to hydrochloric acid?

2 What does an indicator do to show the difference between acid and alkali?

3 What does hydrochloric acid do to the colour of litmus?

4 What colour does litmus go in an alkali?

5 Is water acid, alkali or neutral?
Give a reason for your answer.

7E.3

1 Which indicator, litmus or universal indicator, can you use to tell how strong an acid or alkali is?

2 What colour does universal indicator go in a liquid that is a strong alkali?

3 What does the pH scale measure?

4 Universal indicator goes green in water.
What does this tell us about water?

5 What type of liquid gives a pH of 2?

6 How does the pH number of ammonia solution tell you it is the most alkaline substance shown in the table?

7E.4

1   What is the name of the reaction in which an acid and an alkali cancel each other out?

2   If you add too much acid to an alkali, is the result acidic or alkaline?

3   What colour is the solution next to the washing soda crystal?

4   Are washing soda crystals acidic or alkaline?

5   What is the pH at the top of the test tube?

6   Which section of the tube is the most acidic, the yellow or the red? Give a reason for your answer.

7E.5

1   What causes indigestion?

2   Why must the alkali in indigestion medicine be weak?

3   **a**   Which tablet neutralises the most acid?

    b   Which is the cheapest tablet?

    c   Which tablet works more slowly than all the others?

4   Your saliva is slightly alkaline. What effect will saliva have on the acid in your mouth?

5   What is the name of the gas that makes the bubbles in sponge cakes?

6   What do Scandinavian countries put into lakes and rivers to stop them getting acidic?

7E.HSW

1   Why is group B's method better than group A's?

2   What conclusion can you draw from group B's experiment?

3   What do the pupils in the diagram need to do to work in a safer manner?

4   Use the Internet or some bottle labels to find out the hazards of oven cleaner and bleach.

5   Some hazards are so common that it might be worth putting them in a set of laboratory rules so you don't have to keep putting the same ones in every risk assessment.
Write a set of laboratory rules to cover what you think are the main points for most experiments.

6   What emergency action would you talk to deal with this accident?

7   Write a risk assessment for the experiment the pupil is doing.

- List the substances used and the actions she is carrying out.

- State the hazard for each one.

- State what she should do to reduce the hazard.

(Hint: there are some things she could do to be safer even though, in this picture, these things are not involved.)

7F.1 Chemical reactions

You should already know

Outcomes

Keywords

In a **chemical reaction**, new substances are made.

Chemical reactions happen everywhere:

- when you cook food;
- when plants grow;
- inside your body to keep you alive.

If you cook an egg, the substances in it change into new substances. It is an example of a chemical reaction.

A raw egg in a pan.

The cooked egg is hard and tastes different too.

Question 1

What else happens in a chemical reaction

Other things can happen in a chemical reaction apart from getting a new substance. You can get:

- a colour change – this happens when iron rusts;
- heat;
- a change of pH.

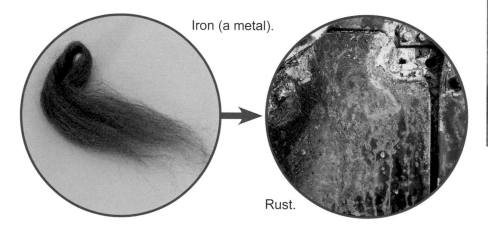

Iron (a metal).

Rust.

Potassium reacting with water.

When potassium is put onto water, it produces hydrogen gas. The reaction produces enough heat to make the hydrogen burn.

If you test the water after the potassium has reacted with it, you find a change of pH from neutral to alkaline.

dropper containing universal indicator

The indicator turns purple, which shows that the solution is alkaline.

Question 2

Burning

When something burns, it reacts with the **oxygen** in the air. New substances are formed.

Burning is a chemical reaction.

One of the new substances formed is usually called an **oxide**.

The oxide formed when natural gas burns is called carbon dioxide.

Burning natural gas in air.

Question 3

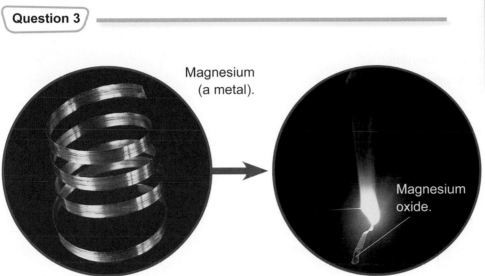

Magnesium
(a metal).

Magnesium
oxide.

When magnesium burns, it reacts with the oxygen in the air.

It makes a new substance called magnesium oxide.

Magnesium oxide is a white, powdery solid.

When carbon burns, it produces a gas called carbon dioxide.

Not all oxides are solids.

Carbon (a non-metal).

Carbon dioxide.

Question 4

You should already know ⟩   Outcomes   ⟩   Keywords ⟩

The pictures show an experiment.

The experiment is a chemical reaction.

- Magnesium reacts with hydrochloric acid.
- A gas is produced.
- The gas is **hydrogen**. It is a new substance.
- The magnesium gradually gets smaller. It disappears.
- This is called **corrosion**.

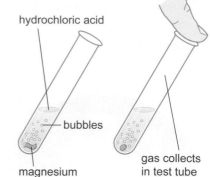

To see the new substance, called magnesium chloride, you leave the tube open for a few days.

- The solution evaporates.
- Solid magnesium chloride is left behind.

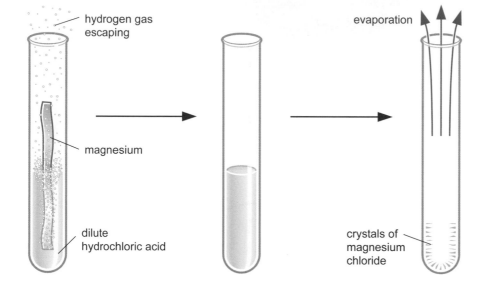

In the experiment, magnesium and hydrochloric acid react together. We call them **reactants**.

The new substances produced are hydrogen and magnesium chloride. We call them **products**.

Question 1 ⟩ ⟨ 2 ⟩

When a metal reacts with an acid:

- one of the products is hydrogen;
- the other new material is called a **salt**.

To make the salt called magnesium chloride, you react magnesium with hydrochloric acid. The diagram shows you the steps.

- Add more magnesium than you need to make sure all the acid is used up.
- Leave it until the reaction has finished. This is when it stops producing a gas.
- Filter off the left over magnesium.
- The products are water and magnesium chloride.
- The magnesium chloride is dissolved in the water so you need to evaporate it to get the salt magnesium chloride.

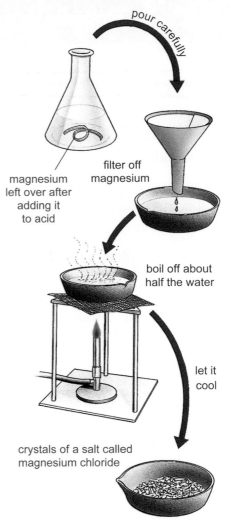

Metal	Acid	Salt
magnesium	hydrochloric acid	magnesium chloride
zinc	hydrochloric acid	zinc chloride
iron	hydrochloric acid	iron chloride

Different combinations of metals and hydrochloric acid make different salts.

Zinc chloride gets its first name from zinc because it was the metal used. It gets its second name from the acid used, which was hydrochloric acid.

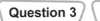

Question 3 **4**

The test for hydrogen gas is shown in the picture.

Hydrogen gas makes a squeaky pop when it burns.

You need to put a lit splint near the mouth of the test tube.

Hydrogen gas is a lot lighter than air. You need to keep a finger or thumb over the test tube to trap the gas before you test it.

If you let the hydrogen escape, there will be none to test!

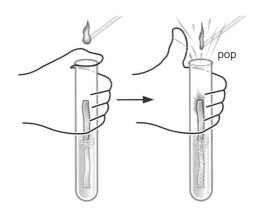

hydrogen + oxygen → water

Question 5

Testing hydrogen gas with a lighted splint.

You should already know   Outcomes   Keywords

Many of the rocks in the Earth contain substances called **carbonates**.

You can test a rock to see whether it has carbonates in it. You put acid on the rock. If there are carbonates in it, it will fizz and produce a gas.

The gas is called **carbon dioxide**.

The top picture shows a rock called limestone in some acid.

It is producing carbon dioxide gas when it reacts with the acid.

Chalk is another rock made from calcium carbonate. When you put acid on chalk there is a reaction. Carbon dioxide is produced.

Limestone is made of calcium carbonate.

Question 1 **2** ——————————

The air contains some carbon dioxide. People increase the amount of carbon dioxide in the air by:

- travelling on an aircraft;
- using a car;
- using electricity.

Carbon dioxide reacts with rainwater to make a very weak acid. This is called **acid rain**.

Over years and years, acid rain can damage buildings.

Some buildings are made from limestone. These are damaged when the acid rain reacts with the limestone.

The photographs show the effect on York Minster. After years of weak acid attacking the limestone, it needs to be restored to what it was like when it was built.

Stonework on York Minster before (left) and after (right) restoration.

Question 3 ——————————

Carbon dioxide is an important gas. It is produced when:

- acid reacts with carbonates;
- things burn;
- living things respire, which is all the time!

The test for carbon dioxide is different from the test for hydrogen.

If you bubble carbon dioxide through **lime water**, the lime water goes cloudy. Carbon dioxide is the only gas that does this.

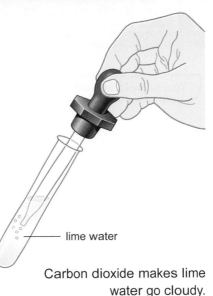

Carbon dioxide makes lime water go cloudy.

When you breathe out, your breath contains more carbon dioxide than the air you breathe in. This is because the cells in your body make carbon dioxide as part of the living processes called **respiration**.

You can test this with a straw and some lime water. If you blow through the lime water with a straw, it will go cloudy.

carbon dioxide (from your breath)

lime water

lime water

white clouds form as gas bubbles through

Question 4 5
Question 4 5

Using carbonates at home

To make light fluffy cakes, you need to get small bubbles inside the cake as it cooks. One way of doing this is to use a substance called baking powder.

Baking powder is a mixture of two white powders called tartaric acid and sodium bicarbonate. They don't react when they are dry.

When you use baking powder in a cake, it produces small bubbles of carbon dioxide gas.

As the cake cooks, the trapped bubbles get bigger and make the cake light and fluffy.

Another way of doing the same thing is to use self-raising flour in a cake. This is flour that has some baking powder already added to it so that it will make carbon dioxide bubbles in the cake mixture.

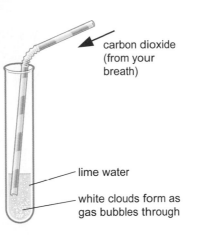

part of cake, magnified

carbon dioxide gas

baking powder in the cake mix

bake

cake

Question 6 7

Check your progress

7F   Simple chemical reactions   85

You should already know | Outcomes | Keywords

Fuels

We burn some substances because they produce heat. We call them **fuels**.

You need three things to make a fire:

- a fuel;
- oxygen from the air;
- heat to get the fuel burning.

When the fire is lit, it produces light and more heat.

The three things needed for a fire are like the sides of a triangle.

When you take away one of the sides, the fire goes out.

The triangle is called the **fire triangle**.

Fire-fighters use water to cool substances.

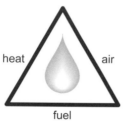

heat   air

fuel

Question 1 **2**

Coal, oil and petrol are called **fossil fuels**. They contain a lot of carbon and its compounds.

They come from the remains of plants and animals that died millions of years ago.

Burning fossil fuels increases the level of carbon dioxide in the air.

Natural gas is a common fossil fuel.

The chemical name for natural gas is **methane**.

This is the gas used in Bunsen burners and domestic cookers.

Burning natural gas in air.

Question 3 **4**

Wax is a fuel

A candle uses wax as its fuel. Wax is a solid. It has to be turned into a gas before it will burn.

Another word for the gas you get from heating something is a vapour.

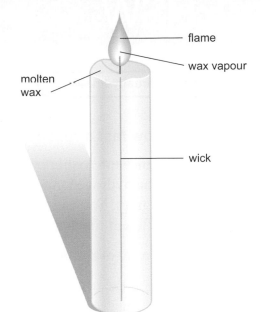

When you light a candle:

- the heat from the flame melts the wax;
- the wick soaks up the molten wax;
- the flame turns the molten wax into wax vapour;
- the wax vapour mixes with air and burns;
- this produces carbon particles that glow yellow in the heat;
- as more air mixes in, the carbon also burns.

You can put a candle out by covering it with a jar.

The candle burns for about half a minute. The flame then gets weaker and goes out.

The candle goes out because it has used up the oxygen inside the jar and produced carbon dioxide.

At first, the candle
continues to burn.

After about 20 seconds,
the candle is still burning.

After about 30 seconds,
the candle goes out.

The jar is full of air to start with. Air is a mixture of gases. There is 21% oxygen, which is used in the burning reaction, and the rest is mostly nitrogen with a little bit of carbon dioxide and argon. Nitrogen, carbon dioxide and argon do not take part in burning. If there is no oxygen or if oxygen cannot get to a flame then it will go out.

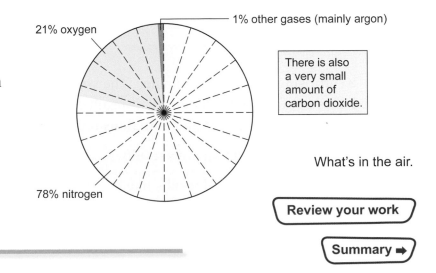

There is also a very small amount of carbon dioxide.

What's in the air.

Review your work

Question 5 6

Summary ➡

| You should already know | Outcomes | Keywords |

Measuring how fast a reaction happens

If you add magnesium to dilute acid, hydrogen gas is produced. The hydrogen gas will push the syringe back in the diagram. You can measure how much gas is produced at different times in the experiment.

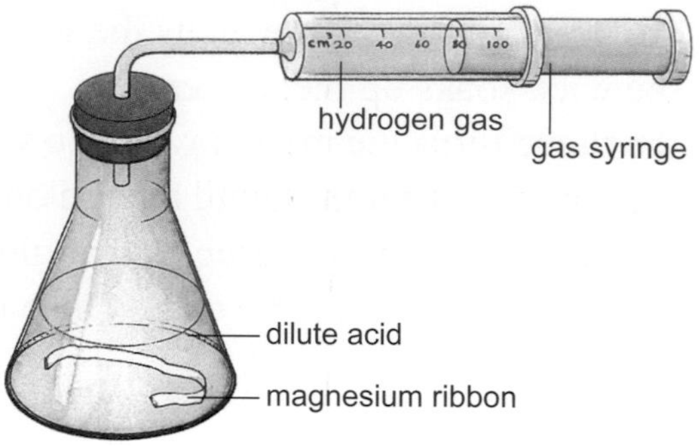

You might get a set of results like those in the table.

Just by looking at the results in the table, you can see something important. After 4 minutes, the reaction has finished.

hydrogen gas

gas syringe

dilute acid

magnesium ribbon

Question 1 | 2

To look at the results more carefully you must plot a graph. The graph is shown below the table.

reaction is slowing down here

reaction is over

no more gas is produced now

reaction is fast at the start

Time (minutes)	Total volume of gas produced (cm³)
0	0
0.5	15
1	30
1.5	38
2	60
2.5	70
3	76
3.5	79
4	80
4.5	80
5	80

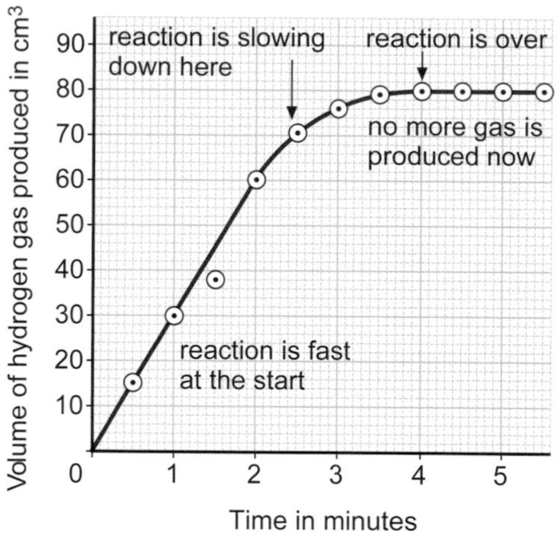

There is a surprising result at 1.5 minutes. The volume of gas produced does not fit into the pattern. This result could be a mistake or an **error**. It is called an **anomalous** result.

The graph helps you spot anomalous results.

When scientists get unexpected results like this, they go back and check them.

Question 3 | 4

Surprising results are not always wrong

Sometimes the result of an experiment is surprising but not an error.

If you do the experiment shown in the diagram, you will get a surprising result.

After the magnesium has burned, the ash left is heavier than the magnesium was to start with!

This type of observation was made in 1772 by the French chemist Antoine Lavoisier. At the time, everyone thought the ashes from something that burned should be lighter because:

- ashes are usually smaller than the substance that burned;
- flames have been seen escaping from the substance – it looks like something has left the original material.

Lavoisier worked out that the ashes being heavier was not a mistake. He did experiments for years with different substances to test his ideas. In 1779 he proposed that, when something burned, it combined with a gas that was in the air. This explained why the ash was heavier. Burning was not something escaping from the substance. It was something combining with it.

He worked out that the part of the air taking part in burning was the part we use up in respiration. He gave it the name <u>oxygen</u>.

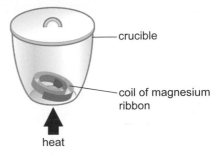

When we heat magnesium in air, we have to lift the lid to allow oxygen in.

> Question 5

Accidental discoveries with sweet results

Sometimes a scientist discover something by accident.

In 1879, Ira Rensen and Constantin Fahlberg accidentally discovered a substance called saccharin.

Saccharin is 300 times sweeter than sugar and it does not make you put on weight like sugar does. We use it today as an artificial sweetener

Fahlberg claimed he spilt the substance on his hand and accidentally licked it. Rensen claimed he forgot to wash his hands after work and noticed a bread roll he was eating later tasted very sweet. We don't know which of them is telling the truth. In any case, the discovery of saccharin as a sweetener was not planned!

Antoine Lavoisier lived during the French Revolution. It was a time when many old ideas and theories were challenged.

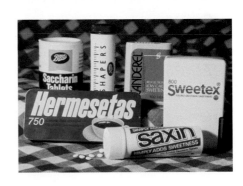

> Question 6

7F.1

1 Give an example of a chemical reaction.

2 What does the reaction between potassium and water produce?

3 What gas in the air does a substance combine with when it burns?

4 What gas does carbon produce when it burns?

7F.2

1 What is the name of the gas produced in the reaction between magnesium and hydrochloric acid?

2 Describe what you see when magnesium corrodes in an acid.

3 Which metal is used to make zinc chloride?

4 Which acid is used to make iron chloride?

5 If you hold a flame near the open end of a test tube of hydrogen, what will happen?

7F.3

1 Which gas is produced when acid is put on a carbonate?

2 What is the name of the carbonate in limestone and chalk?

3 What type of substance is produced when carbon dioxide dissolves in rainwater?

4 Describe the test for carbon dioxide.

5 Why does lime water go cloudy when you breathe into it?

6 What gas does baking powder produce?

7 How does baking powder help in making cakes?

7F.4

1   What is the name for something that burns to produce heat?

2   What <u>three</u> things must you have present to keep a fire burning?

3   What is a fossil fuel? Give some examples.

4   What is the chemical name for natural gas?

5   Why does the candle under the beaker go out?

6   Name some of the gases in the mixture we call air.

7F.HSW

1   How can you tell from the results table that the reaction has finished after 4 minutes?

2   If the experiment makes more than $100\,cm^3$ of gas, the glass plunger of the syringe might fall out. What is the hazard if this happens. What could you do to reduce the hazard?

3   Which of the results is anomalous?

4   If your experiment produced an anomalous result like the one shown, what could you do about it?

5   Find out the key facts about Lavoisier and produce a short presentation about him using ICT.

6   Find out the E number that is given to saccharine and draw up a list of common foods you can buy in the supermarket that contain it.

You should already know

Outcomes

Keywords

All the substances we can see and feel are called **matter**. Gold, leaves, brick, air and water are all examples of matter.

Scientists sort matter into **solid**, **liquid** and **gas**.

These three groups are called the three **states of matter**.

Steel is a solid.

Meths is a purple liquid.

Nitrogen dioxide is a brown gas.

Question 1

State of matter	Shape	Volume
solid	stays the same unless you use a lot of heat or force	stays the same unless you use a lot of heat or force
liquid	fits the shape of the container you put it in up to the level it reaches	stays the same unless you use a lot of heat or force
gas	moves to fit any closed container you put it in	spreads out to fill any space

Solids, liquids and gases behave in different ways.

Liquids can be poured and can move through gaps.

Gases flow like liquids. They are very easy to squash.

Gases spread out to fill any space, like the brown gas in the diagram.

Gases are light for their size.

A suitcase full of air is a lot lighter than one full of gold!

Question 2 3

Matter behaves in a lot of different ways. Scientists try to explain this.

- Liquids and gases flow but solids do not.
- Substances can change from liquid to solid if you cool them.
- Liquids like water change into a gas if you heat them.
- You can smell perfume and air freshener from across a room.
- A tube of gas can be squashed.
- Some substances get bigger when you heat them.
- Some substances can be stretched and then spring back.
- Some substances are heavier than others.

On a snowy day, Sadia gets her milk from the doorstep.

It is cold and the top of the milk is frozen solid.

Sadia cannot pour the milk because the top is frozen.

Some substances can be squashed.

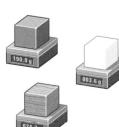

Some substances get longer.

You can smell the gas given off by the air freshener.

0 °C   100 °C

Some substances get bigger as you heat them.

190.0 g   003.6 g   024.3 g

Some substances are heavier than others.

Question 4

Scientists look at what matter does.

They think of ideas to explain what they see. These ideas are called **theories**.

The best theory that explains how matter behaves uses the idea of particles.

Scientists think they can explain how matter behaves if it is made up of a lot of very tiny particles in different arrangements.

Question 5

Scientists discuss and argue about ideas all the time.

You should already know

Outcomes

Keywords

Scientists think all matter is made from very small **particles**.

The particles are too small to see with a normal microscope.

You can get a picture of them using a beam of tiny particles called electrons.

Question 1

The particles are incredibly small. They are invisible.

You can tell the particles are there if you look at grains of dust in the air.

You can see the dust grain being knocked about even though you cannot see the particles that are doing it. The diagram shows you how.

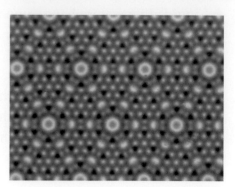

A photograph of particles from a crystal of silicon. This photograph was taken using an electron beam.

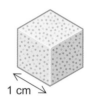

1 cm

A 1 cm³ cube of air contains about 30 million million million particles (30×10^{18}).

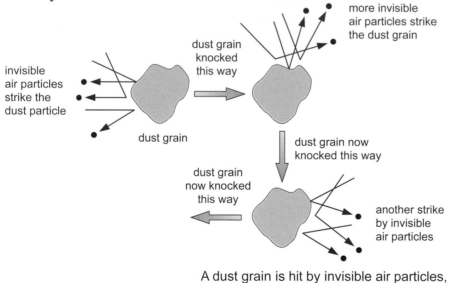

A dust grain is hit by invisible air particles, making it jiggle about in a random way.

If you look at pollen grains in water, you see the same thing happening.

This shows water is made of invisible particles, always on the move.

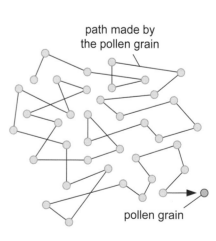

The path of a pollen grain that is jiggling about.

Question 2

Particles in solids, liquids and gases

Solids, liquids and gases are all made up of particles.

In a solid, the particles:

- hold each other together strongly – they are tightly packed;
- **vibrate** – they jiggle about from side to side but they don't change places.

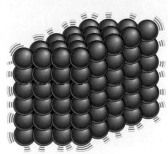

In solids, the particles vibrate while staying in their places.

In liquids, the particles are:

- very close together;
- always moving;
- able to swap places with each other.

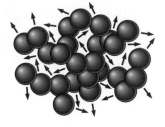

In liquids, the particles still vibrate. They are attracted to each other less than in a solid. This means that they can swap places with each other.

Question 3 **4**

The particles in a gas are:

- far apart;
- a long way from each other, flying about;
- bouncing off each other and anything in their way, like the walls of the container they are in.

A typical air particle in the air on a summer's day will be moving at about 500 metres per second!

Because the particles in a gas are spread out, it is easy to squash a gas.

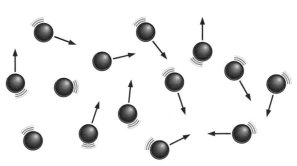

Gases spread out to fill their container.

Solids cannot flow. Liquids and gases can flow, and gases are able to spread into any space. The drawings show how the particle model explains this.

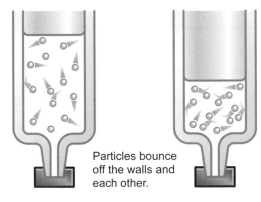

Particles bounce off the walls and each other.

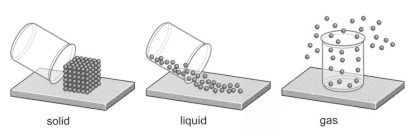

solid   liquid   gas

Solids cannot flow. Liquids and gases can flow. Gases can spread out.

A gas is mostly empty space, so you can squeeze the particles into a smaller space.

Question 5 **6**    **Check your progress**

You should already know   Outcomes   Keywords

Particles in crystals

Many solids are made up of crystals.

Crystals have straight edges.

The photograph shows some copper sulfate crystals. The diagram shows how the particles line up to make the crystals.

Look at the straight edges of these crystals.

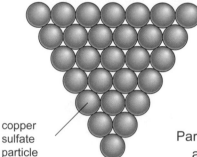

copper sulfate particle

Particles line up to give a neat straight edge.

The copper sulfate particles stick together in a block like a pack of snooker balls.

Question 1

Trying to squash solids, liquids and gases

Another word for 'squash' is '**compress**'.

Solids and liquids are very hard to compress. They do not squash easily.

Gases are easy to compress. The particle idea explains this.

This idea is used in car safety.

An air bag will inflate in front of the driver in a crash. The driver hits a cushion of air which squashes.

This prevents injury.

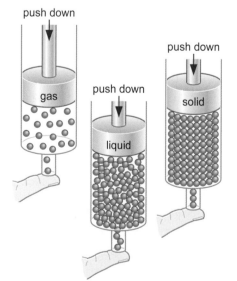

Only gases have enough space between their particles to allow them to be squashed a lot when you compress them.

Question 2

Melting, boiling, freezing and condensing

If you heat a solid it can **melt**.

- Heat makes the particles vibrate faster.
- The particles start to swap places.
- The solid melts into a liquid.

If you heat a liquid it will **evaporate**.

- The particles move faster.
- They break free from each other.
- A gas is formed.

If you heat a liquid enough, the evaporation makes bubbles inside the liquid. We call this boiling.

Condensing is the name for a gas changing to a liquid. The cloud coming from a kettle is the steam condensing to water droplets in the cool air. **Freezing** is the name for a liquid changing to a solid.

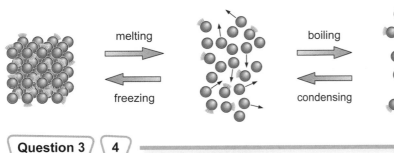

melting · freezing · boiling · condensing

Question 3 **4**

Some things are heavier than others

Solid	Mass of a centimetre cube in grams
lead	11
steel	8
aluminium	3
brass	9

The masses of a centimetre cube of some different metals.

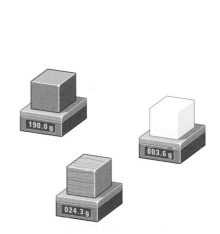

Some substances are heavier than others.

A cubic centimetre of aluminium is a lot lighter than a cubic centimetre of the other metals.

The individual particles in aluminium are lighter than the particles in the other metals. Metals like aluminium are used to make racing cycles as light as possible.

Question 5

You should already know

Outcomes

Keywords

Diffusion

Liquids and gases can spread out without any help from the wind, water currents or stirring. We call this spreading out **diffusion**.

Put a drop of ink or a coloured crystal into some still water.

The colour spreads slowly through the water. It sometimes takes a few weeks!

A gas does the same thing more quickly.

Gas particles have a lot of space between each other and fly about very fast.

The brown gas in the diagram spreads into the whole space in about 10 minutes.

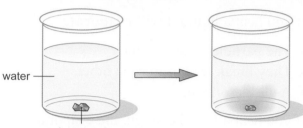

water

purple potassium permanganate crystal

The purple dye diffuses through the water.

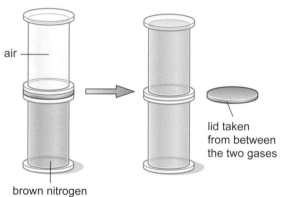

air

brown nitrogen dioxide gas

lid taken from between the two gases

The gases spread out.

Question 1

Hydrochloric acid produces a gas. So does ammonia. The two gases react when they meet. They make a white substance called ammonium chloride.

Ammonia gas particles move faster than the particles of hydrogen chloride gas. This means the ammonium chloride is nearer the left end of the tube.

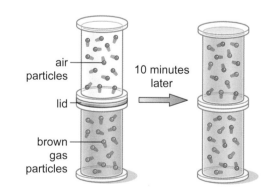

air particles

lid

brown gas particles

10 minutes later

The gas particles are moving, so they mix. We say that they diffuse.

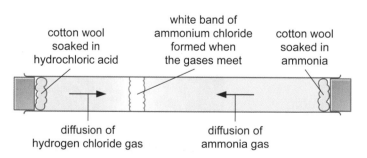

cotton wool soaked in hydrochloric acid

white band of ammonium chloride formed when the gases meet

cotton wool soaked in ammonia

diffusion of hydrogen chloride gas

diffusion of ammonia gas

The two transparent gases diffuse. They form a white cloud when they meet. Both of the gases have particles that are moving.

Question 2

Crushing a can with air particles

Heat a can containing a small amount of water. When lots of steam has come out, put the lid on and leave it to cool.

- The water boils and makes steam.
- The steam forces out the air particles that were inside the can.
- When the top is put back on, the air cannot get back inside.
- When the can cools, the steam condenses.
- Liquid water takes up less space than steam.
- There are more air particles hitting the outside than the inside.
- The force of the air particles on the outside crushes the can.

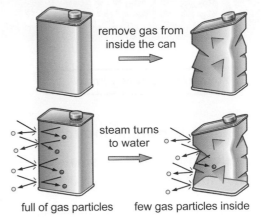

remove gas from inside the can

steam turns to water

full of gas particles   few gas particles inside

The can is crushed because more particles are hitting the outside than the inside of the can.

Question 3

Heat conduction in solids

Heat travels through the metal of the spoon. Particles at high temperature vibrate faster and the vibrations pass from particle to particle through the spoon. The top of the spoon gets hot.

We call this **conduction** of heat.

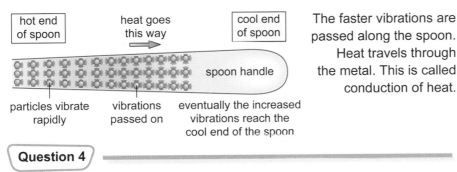

hot end of spoon   heat goes this way   cool end of spoon

spoon handle

particles vibrate rapidly   vibrations passed on   eventually the increased vibrations reach the cool end of the spoon

The faster vibrations are passed along the spoon. Heat travels through the metal. This is called conduction of heat.

Question 4

Expansion means getting bigger. Solids expand a bit when you heat them. Liquids expand more. Gases expand a lot.

A substance expands because the particles move faster when they get hotter and take up more space. This effect is used in thermometers filled with mercury.

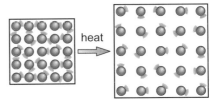

heat

The particles move further apart when they vibrate more.

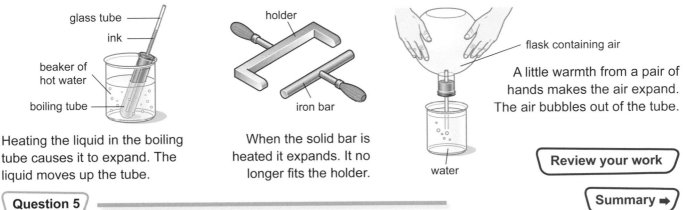

glass tube

ink

beaker of hot water

boiling tube

holder

iron bar

flask containing air

water

Heating the liquid in the boiling tube causes it to expand. The liquid moves up the tube.

When the solid bar is heated it expands. It no longer fits the holder.

A little warmth from a pair of hands makes the air expand. The air bubbles out of the tube.

Review your work

Question 5

Summary ➡

You should already know | Outcomes | Keywords

What is Brownian motion?

Pollen grains are very small and light. If you mix them in water, they float about like dust does in the air.

If you look through a microscope at pollen floating about in water you see that:

- the pollen grains are jiggling about with no pattern;
- they are always moving in a zigzag manner.

The first person to notice this was a Scottish biologist called Robert Brown, in 1827. It is called **Brownian motion**.

Testing an explanation

Robert Brown tried to explain what he saw.

He suggested that the pollen grains were alive because they had come from a plant. Being alive made them move.

To tested his idea, he looked at something similar that he knew could not be alive. He looked at some dirt in some water trapped in a lump of transparent rock called quartz. The water had been trapped in the quartz for millions of years.

When he looked at the water, the dirt was jiggling about just like the pollen grains.

The dirt could not be alive. It had been trapped in the quartz for too long. Brown's second observation showed that his explanation was wrong

Brown did not manage to explain Brownian motion.

Robert Brown (1773–1858).

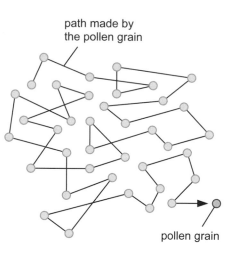

path made by the pollen grain

pollen grain

The path of a pollen grain that is jiggling about.

Question 1 | 2 | 3

More observations

Between 1827 and 1900, other scientists from other countries and other branches of science made observations of Brownian motion.

By 1900, scientists knew that:

- the speed of Brownian motion depends on the size of the particle – small particles jiggle faster than larger ones;
- particles jiggled faster if the liquid or gas they were in was hotter;
- there is no pattern to the jiggling – it is random;
- you can see Brownian motion of dust particles in the air.

These observations fitted in with the **particle model of matter**, which was being worked out from about 1870 onwards.

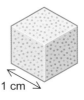

A 1 cm³ cube of air contains about 30 million million million particles (3×10^{19}).

In the particle model of matter, air and water are made up of millions of invisible particles. These are always moving. This makes dust or pollen particles jiggle about because they are knocked about by the invisible particles of air or water. The diagram shows the idea.

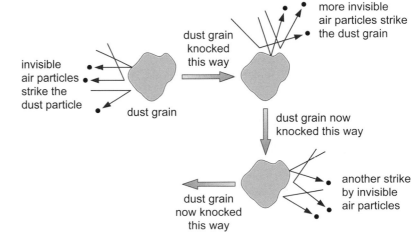

Question 4 **5** ─────────────────

A dust grain is his by invisible air particles, making it jiggle about in a random way.

Albert Einstein

In 1905, Albert Einstein worked out a mathematical theory about Brownian motion. It was tested by experiments. Tests showed that his ideas worked. From these tests, a French scientist called Jean Perrin worked out the size and mass of the invisible particles that make up matter.

This finally convinced everybody that the particle model of matter was correct, even though the particles were invisible.

This is an example of how science develops when people share and work on ideas from different areas like maths and science.

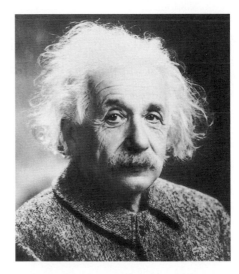

Albert Einstein, mathematician and physicist (1879–1955).

Question 6 ─────────────────

7G.1

1 What are the <u>three</u> states of matter?
2 Give examples of a solid, a liquid and a gas.
3 How does the shape of a solid compare with the shape of a gas?
4 What does a liquid like water do if you heat it?
5 What do scientists think all matter is made from?

7G.2

1 What do scientists think all matter is made from?
2 What makes dust particles jiggle about in the air?
3 What does 'vibrate' mean?
4 How are the particles arranged in a liquid?
5 How are the particles arranged in a gas?
6 Name <u>one</u> thing that gases and liquids can do that solids cannot do.

7G.3

1 How can you use ideas about particles to explain the straight edge of a crystal?
2 Why are gases easy to squash?
3 What happens to the particles when a solid melts?
4 What happens to the particles when a liquid boils?
5 Where is a light metal like aluminium useful?

7G.4

1 What is the name for dye spreading through water on its own without being stirred?

2 What is the name of the product when hydrogen chloride gas reacts with ammonia gas?

3 What forces the air particles out of the can?

4 Why does the handle of a spoon get hot when it is stood in a hot drink?

5 Describe how you could show that something expands when it gets hotter.

7G.HSW

1 What observations did Brown make that were surprising?

2 How did Brown know that his explanation of the observation was wrong?

3 Search the Internet for information on Robert Brown and put together a short presentation about him including at least one of the other important things he did.

4 How can the particle model of matter explain the observation of Brownian motion?

5 Why would pollen grains be made to jiggle faster if the water they are in is heated up?

6 Albert Einstein worked in many different parts of the world during his life and was responsible for many important things.
Research Einstein on the internet and construct a timeline of the important dates, including where he lived and worked, and his most significant discoveries.

If you spill water on an exercise book, the ink might 'run' but the pencil doesn't. Water dissolves some types of ink. It does not dissolve pencil.

Put salt into a beaker of water and the salt vanishes.

Do the same with sand and it just sinks to the bottom.

The salt dissolves in the water. We say that salt is **soluble** in water.

Sand does not dissolve in water. We say that sand is **insoluble** in water.

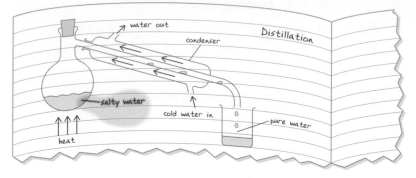

You can still see the sand, but the salt seems to have vanished.

When the salt dissolves in the water it makes a **solution**.

- The salt is called the **solute** – it is the solid that **dissolves**.
- The water is called the **solvent** – it is the liquid that dissolves the solid.

Both the salt solution and the sand and water are **mixtures** of substances.

salt + water → salt solution

solute + solvent → solution

Question 1 2

Everyday mixtures

A scientist would not describe mineral water as 'pure'.
The mineral water contains a lot of different minerals
dissolved in water.

It is a mixture.

The label has a list of substances dissolved in the water.

In science the word 'pure' means something only contains a single
substance. A pure substance is not a mixture of substances.

Mixtures are found everywhere.

- Mineral water is a mixture of water and dissolved minerals.
- Coffee is a mixture of water and coffee. Some people add milk
  or sugar when they drink it.
- Sea water is a mixture of water and dissolved salt.

AQUA SPRING
Natural Mineral Water

Amounts of dissolved minerals (mg/litre)

calcium	35.0
magnesium	8.0
sodium	6.5
hydrogencarbonate	124.0
chloride	6.5
sulfate	6.0

> **Question 3** **4**

Separating a mixture of sand and water

Sand can be separated from the water using a method called
filtration.

The sand and water mixture is poured through a filter paper. The
filter paper has very tiny holes, too small to see. It acts like a very
fine sieve.

The water goes through the tiny holes in the paper.

The sand does not go through. It is trapped on the paper. You can
see sand particles. They are much larger than the holes in the paper.

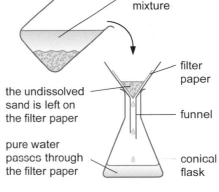

Separating sand and water.

> **Question 5**

Separating a mixture of salt and water

Salt water is a mixture of salt and water. The salt is dissolved in the
water. Filtering does not work. Particles of dissolved salt are smaller
than the holes in the filter paper.

The salt is separated from the water by **evaporation**.

When you heat the salt solution, the water evaporates into the air.

The salt does not evaporate. It is left behind on the evaporating dish.

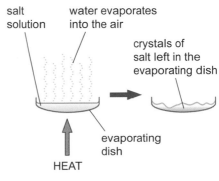

Separating salt and water.

> **Question 6**

You should already know | Outcomes | Keywords

The chemical name for salt is **sodium chloride**.

Sodium chloride is often called 'common salt'.

We find it in:

- some types of rock – this is called rock salt;
- sea water – it contains a lot of salt.

Salt is taken out of rocks or sea water all over the world.

Crushed rock salt.

In the UK, water is pumped into the rock salt. The salt dissolves and salt solution is pumped to the surface.

In Australia, sea water is collected. Sunlight is used to evaporate the water until salt crystals form.

In the USA, rock salt is mined by cutting, drilling and blasting.

Salt and rock salt have a lot of uses.

Rock salt is crushed and spread on roads in winter. The salt:

- melts snow and ice;
- makes driving safer.

Important chemicals are made from salt. We say salt is an important raw material.

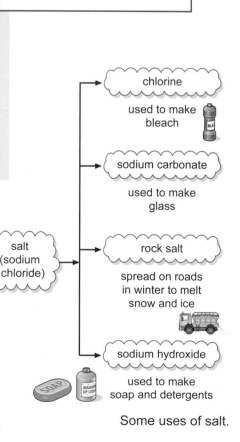

Some uses of salt.

Question 1 | 2

What happens when salt dissolves?

When you dissolve salt in water, you get a colourless solution. The salt crystals disappear.

The salt crystals are made of many millions of very tiny salt particles. When they are held together in a crystal, you can see the crystal.

When the salt crystals are in the water, the tiny particles break away. The tiny salt particles mix in amongst the water particles. The tiny particles are too small to see. The salt crystal disappears. It has dissolved.

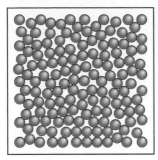  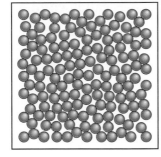

We can see the undissolved salt crystal because the salt particles are packed tightly together.

The water particles smash into the salt particles and break them apart.

The water particles eventually separate all the salt particles. The separate salt particles are too small to be seen, so the solution looks clear.

Question 3   4

You can show that the tiny salt particles are in the water when salt dissolves by using a balance.

solute

solvent

solution

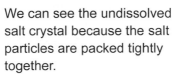  

4 g of salt...

...dissolved in 100 g of water...

...forms 104 g of solution.

The mass of the salt solution is the same as the total mass of the salt (= the solute) and the water (= the solvent). This is true for any solution.

When a solute dissolves it is part of the solution. No mass is lost.

The name for this is **conservation of mass**.

Question 5   6

Getting the solvent back from a solution

Bathroom mirrors steam up when you have a hot bath. Hot steam from the bath hits the cold mirror. The cold mirror cools the steam back into water.

This is called **condensation**.

When you heat a solution made with water, the water **evaporates** as steam.

Other substances can get left behind.

Cold windows and walls make steam change back to water (it condenses).

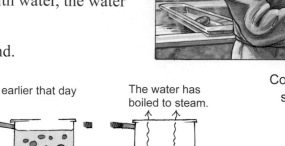

earlier that day   The water has boiled to steam.

solid bits left behind

Question 1

You can get pure water from salty water. You need to cool the steam in a **condenser**. This is a cold tube. The steam goes into it and changes to pure water.

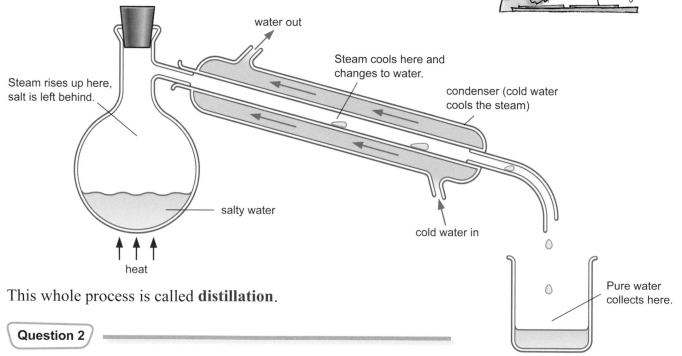

water out

Steam cools here and changes to water.

condenser (cold water cools the steam)

Steam rises up here, salt is left behind.

salty water

cold water in

heat

Pure water collects here.

This whole process is called **distillation**.

Question 2

Chromatography

Black ink is made from different colours mixed together.

We can separate the mixture of colours using **chromatography**.

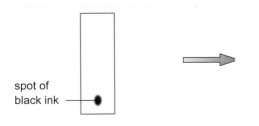 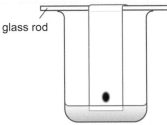

glass rod

spot of
black ink

A spot of black ink is placed
on the chromatography paper.

The paper is suspended in the
water. The spot of ink must be
above the level of the water.

The black ink separates into
different colours. Each colour is
a different solute in the original
ink mixture.

The piece of paper you get at the end of doing chromatography is
called a **chromatogram**.

Question 3

Using chromatography

You can use chromatography to study the dyes used in food.

A pure substance only has one colour on the chromatogram.

The chromatogram shows that the blue and yellow food
colourings are pure substances. They only contain one substance.

The brown food colouring is a mixture of the yellow and blue
colourings with a third colour mixed in.

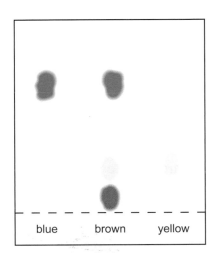

blue   brown   yellow

Chromatography results for blue,
brown and yellow food colourings.

Question 4

Scientists use chromatography in a lot of
situations. These include:

- finding out which pigments are contained
  in leaves;
- comparing the blood of a suspect with blood
  found at the scene of a crime;
- testing urine to check a patient's health.

 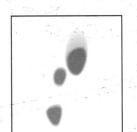

A chromatogram of urine
from a healthy person.

A chromatogram of urine
from a patient suffering
from phenylketonuria.

Question 5

Check your progress

If you add salt to water and stir it, at first the salt vanishes.

After you have added quite a bit of salt, it stops vanishing no matter how much you stir.

No more salt will dissolve. If you keep adding salt it just piles up on the bottom of the beaker.

A solution in which no more solid will dissolve is called a **saturated solution**.

The same thing happens when you put sugar in tea. After a while you cannot make it any sweeter. The tea is a saturated solution. If you add more sugar it just ends up in the bottom of the cup.

Some solids will dissolve in water. We say they are **soluble** in water.

If a solid does not dissolve in water we say it is **insoluble** in water.

To dissolve a solid, you need to use a solvent that will work.

Water does not dissolve everything. For example some types of ink are soluble in alcohol but not in water. To remove graffiti you might have to use a solvent like alcohol.

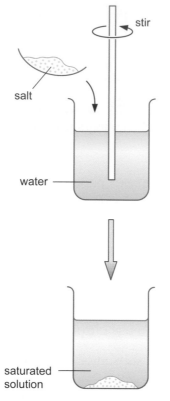

stir

salt

water

saturated solution

Making a saturated solution of salt in water.

Question 1) 2

Stain removers

You can buy different things to dissolve stains on clothes, carpet and furniture.

Different stains dissolve better in different substances. If you want to dissolve an oil stain, you need a stain remover that will work on oil. It must have a solvent in it that will dissolve oil.

Luckily, most common stains dissolve in water with a bit of detergent in it. This is the basis for washing clothes.

Different stains need different stain removers.

Temperature affects how much will dissolve

Things dissolve better if the temperature is higher.

Sugar is easy to dissolve in a cup of hot tea. It is not so easy to dissolve if the tea is cold. You can easily test this out.

- Get two beakers with the same amount of water in.
- Heat one beaker to 20 °C.
- Heat the other beaker to 60 °C.
- Add a spoonful of sugar to each beaker.
- Stir both beakers ten times.
- Add another teaspoonful of sugar to each beaker.
- Stir both beakers again.
- Keep doing this a few times.

You will be able to dissolve more sugar in the hot water than you can in the cold water.

The same idea applies to lots of things. Clothes get cleaner if the water you wash them in is hot.

If you wash up dirty pots in cold water, the dirt and grease are hard to clean off. If you use hot water it is a lot easier.

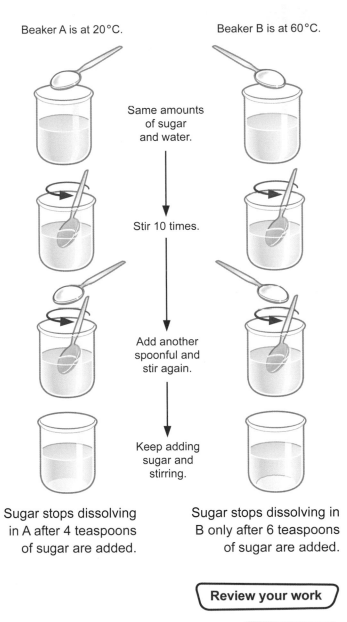

Beaker A is at 20°C.   Beaker B is at 60°C.

Same amounts of sugar and water.

Stir 10 times.

Add another spoonful and stir again.

Keep adding sugar and stirring.

Sugar stops dissolving in A after 4 teaspoons of sugar are added.

Sugar stops dissolving in B only after 6 teaspoons of sugar are added.

Review your work

Question 3 4

Summary ➡

You should already know   Outcomes   Keywords

Dissolving salt in water

A group of pupils are investigating how temperature affects how much salt will dissolve in water. They are discussing **variables**. These are the things that might affect the result and the things they will change and measure.

The volume of water matters.

Yes, we need to keep it the same for a fair test.

Salt dissolves faster in hot water than it does in cold.

We can measure the amount of salt by the number of spatulas we add.

Question 1 ⟩ ⟨2⟩

The pupils use this method.

- Measure out 50 cm³ of water.
- Count the number of spatulas of salt that will dissolve in it.
- Repeat the experiment at a different temperatures.

The variable they will change is the water temperature. This is the input of the experiment. It is called the input variable or the **independent variable**.

They will count the number of spatulas that will dissolve. This is the output of the experiment. It is called the output variable or the **dependent variable**.

The volume of water is a variable that is being kept the same so that the test is fair. This is called a **control variable**.

Question 3 ⟩ ⟨4⟩ ⟨5⟩

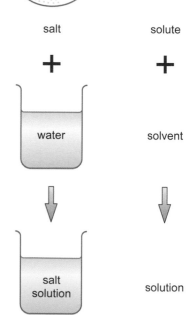

salt   solute

+   +

water   solvent

↓   ↓

salt solution   solution

In the experiment, salt will be added to water to make salt solution.

Rules for plotting a graph

Put the independent variable on the bottom axis.

Put the dependent variable on the side axis.

Label the axes and put in any units (such as °C).

Use fine crosses to mark points.

Analysing results

The students produce a table of results like this.

Temperature of water (°C)	22	31	39	50	61
Number of spatulas of salt	5	6	7	9	12

The results table is good. It has clear headings with units.

The rules for showing the results on a graph are given in the box.

They produce a graph like this one.

It has three mistakes on it before they draw the line!

One of them is that they should have put the temperature on the bottom axis because it is the independent (input) variable.

The number of spatulas is the output of the experiment. This is the dependent (output) variable. It goes on the side axis, not along the bottom.

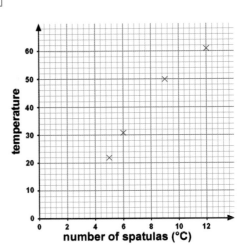

Question 6   7

Here are the results and the graph for another experiment to find out how much salt you can get out of rock salt. The graph is shown before the line is drawn and it already has three mistakes. See if you can spot them!

Mass of rock salt (g)	5	10	15	20	25
Mass of salt extracted (g)	1	3	6	8	10

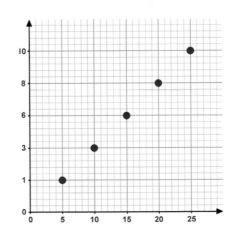

Question 8   9

7H.1

1 How can you tell that sand is not soluble but salt is?

2 What is the name for a liquid that dissolves a solid?

3 What does the word 'pure' mean in science?

4 Give <u>one</u> everyday example of a mixture.

5 Give <u>one</u> example of a mixture that can be separated using filtration.

6 Describe how you could separate a mixture of water and salt.

7H.2

1 What is the chemical name for common salt?

2 Name some important chemicals made from salt.

3 How are the solvent and solute particles arranged in a solution?

4 What can you do to a salt solution to get the salt crystals back?

5 Describe how to show that no mass is lost when you dissolve salt in water.

6 What mass of salt solution is made when you dissolve 7 g of salt in 50 g of water? Explain how you worked out your answer.

7H.3

1 What is the name for the process in which steam cools and changes back into water?

2 What is the name of the process used to get pure water from salt water?

3 Describe how to make a chromatogram.

4 How can chromatography tell you how many different chemicals there are in a food dye?

5 Name <u>three</u> ways in which chromatography is used.

7H.4

1   What is the name for a solution in which no more solid
    will dissolve?

2   What does it mean if you say something is soluble in water?

3   Which will dissolve the most sugar – a hot cup of tea or a cold
    cup of tea?

4   Why is it a good idea to wash up in hot water rather than cold?

7H.HSW

1   Which three variables have the pupils identified?

2   How do you think increasing the volume of water will affect
    how much salt dissolves?
    Give a reason for your answer.

3   Which variable is the independent variable in the pupils'
    experiment?

4   Which variable is a control variable in the pupils' experiment?

5   Which variable is the dependent variable in the pupils' experiment?

6   What are the other mistakes that the pupils have made on the graph?

7   Plot a correct graph of the pupils' results. Remember, the number of
    spatulas needs to go up the side of the graph and the temperature of
    the water goes along the bottom.

8   What three mistakes are shown on the graph?

9   Plot a correct graph of the results given in the table.

71.1 Energy and fuels

We need **energy** to make things happen. We measure it in **joules**.

There are different types of energy.

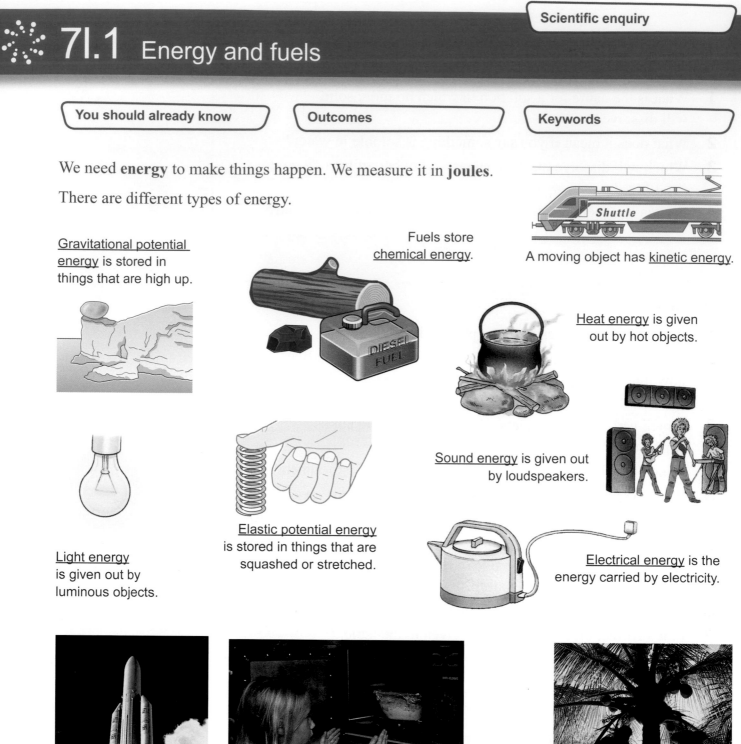

Gravitational potential energy is stored in things that are high up.

Fuels store chemical energy.

A moving object has kinetic energy.

Heat energy is given out by hot objects.

Sound energy is given out by loudspeakers.

Light energy is given out by luminous objects.

Elastic potential energy is stored in things that are squashed or stretched.

Electrical energy is the energy carried by electricity.

The rocket needs energy to take off.

The microwave oven needs energy to cook.

The cheetah needs energy to run.

The plant needs energy to grow.

Question 1 | 2

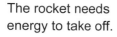

When anything happens, energy changes from one type to another.

We say energy <u>transfers</u> from one type to another. The picture shows the energy transfer for a kettle.

Often, energy transfers into more than one type.

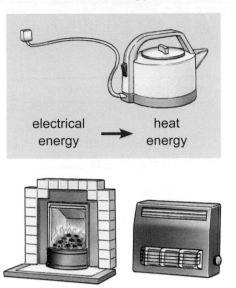

electrical energy → heat energy

What happens	Energy transfer
something burning, like coal or wood	<u>chemical</u> energy transfers to <u>heat</u> and <u>light</u>
an electric fire heating a room	<u>electrical</u> energy transfers to <u>heat</u> and <u>light</u>

Question 3 / 4

Useful fuels

We often get energy by burning things. The things we burn to get energy are called **fuels**.

- Wood burns in a camp fire to cook food.
- Gas burns in a Bunsen burner.
- Petrol burns inside a car engine.
- Wax burns in a candle.

Fuels are stores of chemical energy.

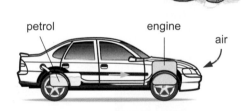

petrol   engine   air

air   air

molten wax

gas   air

Fuels won't burn without oxygen from the air.

Oil is used to heat schools.

Gas is used to cook.

Coal is used to generate electricity.

Aircraft use aviation fuel.

Question 5 / 6

| You should already know | Outcomes | Keywords |

The main fuels used in power stations to make electricity are **coal**, **oil** and **natural gas**.

Coal, oil and gas come from the remains of plants and animals that died millions of years ago. You sometimes see the fossil of a plant in coal.

Coal, oil and gas are called **fossil fuels**.

When the plants were alive they stored energy from the sunlight.

When the plants died they got buried in muddy swamps.

They turned into coal over millions of years.

Nature makes fossil fuels very slowly. We are using fossil fuels very quickly. This means that they will run out some day soon.

We say that fossil fuels are **non-renewable**.

This piece of coal has the fossilised remains of a plant in it.

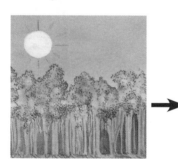 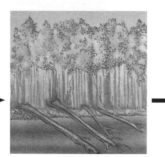 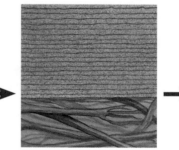 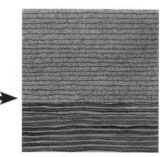

Trees store energy from sunlight as they grow.

Dead trees fall into swamps.

The dead trees are buried under layers of mud.

The wood gradually turns into coal.

How coal was formed.

  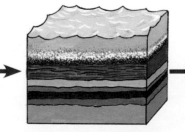 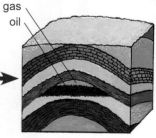

gas
oil

Sea creatures store energy.

These creatures die and sink to the bottom.

The dead creatures are buried under layers of sand.

The creatures gradually turn into oil and gas which are trapped under rock.

How oil and gas were formed.

(Question 1) (2) (3)

We use fossil fuels to make most of our electricity

The electric light bulb was invented in 1879.

Since then, we have used electricity more and more.

These days, most people could not live without electricity.

Fossil fuels are easy to use. Most of our electrical energy comes from the chemical energy in fossil fuels but:

- they cause pollution;
- they will run out.

coal

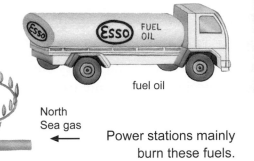
fuel oil

North Sea gas ←

Power stations mainly burn these fuels.

Gases from car exhausts cause air pollution.

Fossil fuel	Advantages	Disadvantages
coal	• reliable • plentiful supply	• needs to be transported and stored • burning it causes acid rain and global warming
mineral oil	• can transport it in pipes	• needs to be transported and stored • bad sea pollution happens when tankers spill oil • burning it causes acid rain and global warming
natural gas	• burns more cleanly than others	• difficult to drill for • needs to be transported and stored • burning it causes acid rain and global warming

It is important to save fossil fuels because

- they are running out
- they cause pollution
- they cause global warning.
- they are useful for making things like plastics.

Fossil fuels can be saved by

- using other ways to make electricity
- using devices like energy efficient light bulbs.

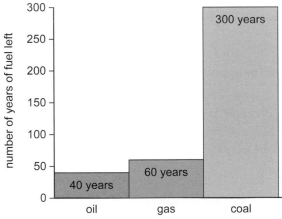

Bar chart showing when fossil fuels will run out, based on current rates of consumption of known world reserves.

Question 4 / 5 _____ Check your progress

You should already know   **Outcomes**   **Keywords**

Fossil fuels will run out one day: they are non-renewable. They also cause global warming.

We need different sources of energy from fossil fuels.

We can get energy from the **wind** and **waves**. This energy will last as long as the sun keeps shining. We say that wind energy and wave energy are **renewable**. This means that they will not run out.

Many renewable energy resources get their energy from the Sun.

The drawing shows how the wind, a wave on the sea and hydro-electric power stations get their energy from the Sun.

The Sun will keep on shining for about 5 billion more years.

So <u>solar</u> energy is a renewable energy resource.

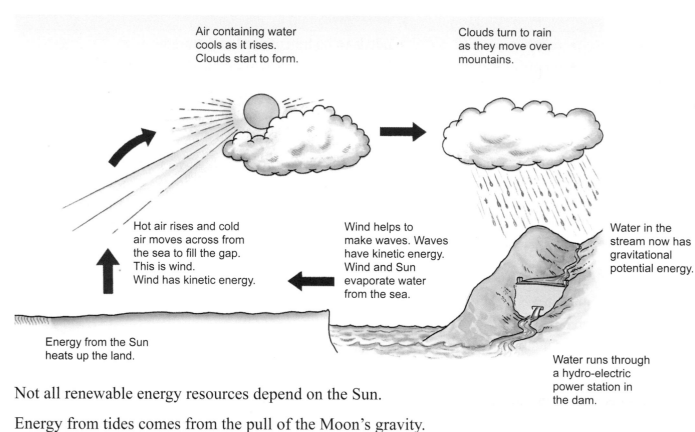

Air containing water cools as it rises. Clouds start to form.

Clouds turn to rain as they move over mountains.

Hot air rises and cold air moves across from the sea to fill the gap. This is wind. Wind has kinetic energy.

Wind helps to make waves. Waves have kinetic energy. Wind and Sun evaporate water from the sea.

Water in the stream now has gravitational potential energy.

Energy from the Sun heats up the land.

Water runs through a hydro-electric power station in the dam.

Not all renewable energy resources depend on the Sun.

Energy from tides comes from the pull of the Moon's gravity. This is called **tidal** energy.

Geothermal energy comes from the heat energy in hot rocks deep underground.

Question 1   **2**   **3**

Biomass energy

Plants trap energy from the Sun. This is called **biomass** energy. You can use plant material as a source of energy. You can burn it or make a liquid fuel from it that can be used in cars.

Biomass is renewable.

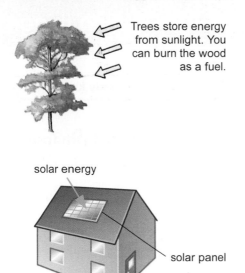

Trees store energy from sunlight. You can burn the wood as a fuel.

Solar energy

Solar <u>cells</u> produce small amounts of electricity. They are used in garden lights and pocket calculators. They are too expensive to use to produce a lot of electricity.

Solar <u>panels</u> use the heat from the Sun to heat water.

Solar energy is renewable.

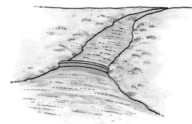

solar energy

solar panel

Solar panels absorb heat from the Sun. They are used to heat water in houses.

Tidal energy

The Moon's gravity causes the tides. Water is trapped behind a barrier at high tide. At low tide, the water flows back through turbines. The turbine drive generators to produce electricity.

Tidal energy is renewable.

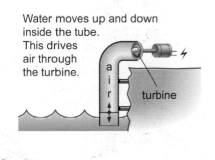

When the barrage is full, the mud flats in the estuary are flooded all the time.

Wind energy

The kinetic energy of the wind is used to turn a turbine. This drives a generator to make electricity.

Turbines only produce electricity when the wind blows. Wind energy is renewable.

Wave energy

Waves are caused when the wind blows on the sea. Waves can push air past a turbine that drives a generator.

This idea has not been fully tried yet. Wave energy is renewable.

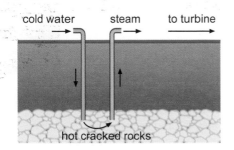

Water moves up and down inside the tube. This drives air through the turbine.

air

turbine

Geothermal energy

The rocks deep underground are hot from the heat produced in the Earth's core.

You can pump water down into cracked rocks and get it back as steam. The steam can be used to drive turbines to make electricity. Geothermal energy is renewable.

cold water   steam   to turbine

hot cracked rocks

Question 4 5 6 7

You should already know

Outcomes

Keywords

We need energy from food for everything we do

All living things use energy.

Animals get energy from the food they eat to live and do things.

Different activities need different amounts of energy. We measure energy in **joules**. A joule isn't a very large measure of energy, so **kilojoules** are often used.

1 kilojoule is 1000 joules.

The pictures show how many kilojoules are needed for different activities.

Jogging needs 60 kilojoules of energy for every minute you jog.

Riding a bike needs 30 kilojoules of energy for every minute you ride.

Walking needs 20 kilojoules of energy for every minute you stroll along.

Sleeping needs 6 kilojoules of energy for every minute you sleep.

Question 1　2　3

Energy from food

Food labels show how much chemical energy is in the food. The labels show the energy in kilojoules (kJ) and an old unit for energy called the kilocalorie (kcal).

If you use more energy in activities than you get from food, you lose weight.

Exercise helps keep weight down.

People who do active jobs, like builders, need more food than people who sit at a desk all day.

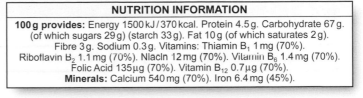

NUTRITION INFORMATION

100 g provides: Energy 1500 kJ / 370 kcal. Protein 4.5 g. Carbohydrate 67 g. (of which sugars 29 g) (starch 33 g). Fat 10 g (of which saturates 2 g). Fibre 3 g. Sodium 0.3 g. Vitamins: Thiamin B_1 1 mg (70%). Riboflavin B_2 1.1 mg (70%). Niacin 12 mg (70%). Vitamin B_6 1.4 mg (70%). Folic Acid 135 µg (70%). Vitamin B_{12} 0.7 µg (70%). **Minerals:** Calcium 540 mg (70%). Iron 6.4 mg (45%).

NUTRITION INFORMATION	PER PIECE	PER 100 g
ENERGY:	1180 kJ / 281 kcal	1885 kJ / 449 kcal
PROTEIN:	2.6 g	4.2 g
CARBOHYDRATE:	43.1 g	69.0 g
FAT:	10.9 g	17.4 g

Nutrition labels.

The energy in food comes from the Sun

Like all living things, plants need food to live and grow.

Plants make their own food. They use the energy in sunlight.

Animals get their energy from eating plants or other animals.

This means that all food energy originally comes from the Sun.

Potato plants use the energy in sunlight to make their food.

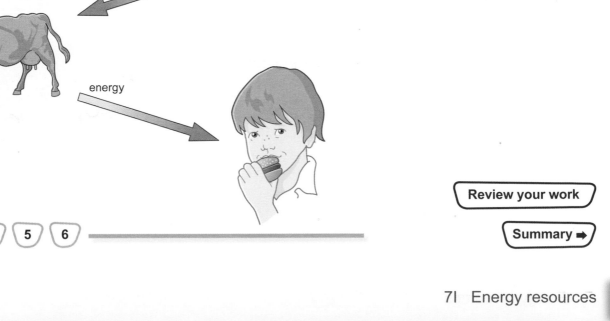

Review your work

Question 4   5   6

Summary ➡

You should already know | Outcomes | Keywords

What are ethical and moral implications?

Some people will think that building a wind farm is a good thing.

- It supplies renewable energy.
- It does not pollute the atmosphere when it is operating.

Other people will object.

- It changes the appearance of the landscape.
- It will create some noise when it operates.

Deciding whether or not to build a wind farm will be a decision based on many things, some for it and some against.

Considering the **ethical** and **moral** implications means thinking about the positive and negative impacts of the decision on the lives of people, plants, animals and the environment in general.

Worn out wind turbines will be relatively cheap to dismantle. They don't contain dangerous materials. Wind farms don't pollute the air with waste gases. But some people object to their appearance and the noise they make. They might be prepared to pay more for electricity to avoid having generators in beauty spots.

Meeting the demand for energy

Our demand for energy is very high. The fossil fuels are running out. Using them causes pollution and global warming. Finding alternatives to diesel and petrol for road transport would help considerably. One idea is to use hydrogen as a fuel.

- Solar cells produce electricity.
- The electricity is used to get the hydrogen out of water, and this is stored in a tank.
- Your car is converted to use hydrogen gas as a fuel.

Using hydrogen as a fuel produces water as the exhaust gas and there is no pollution.

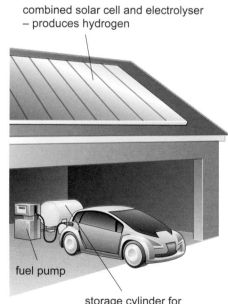

combined solar cell and electrolyser – produces hydrogen

fuel pump

storage cylinder for compressed hydrogen gas

A scheme for powering hydrogen-fuelled cars from sunlight.

Question 1 / 2

Problems to solve

There are problems with the alternatives to fossil fuels. Some of these problems are **technical**. Some are ethical and moral.

Problem	Possible solution
You need six hundred of the most powerful wind turbines operating all the time to produce as much electricity as one coal fired power station.	Make a better design of wind turbine that produces more electricity.
Hydro-electricity does not cause pollution but there are very few hydro-electric sites in the UK.	Flood more areas of land to construct hydro-electric schemes.
Nuclear power stations don't pollute the air but they produce radioactive waste that will be dangerous for thousands of years.	Seal the waste in concrete blocks that will keep it safe for a few hundred years and hope that future generations find a way of dealing with it.

Question 3 4 5 _____

One thing leads to another

In science, a development can produce a new problem that was not expected. An example is the use of power lines.

However we produce electricity, we need to transport it across the country using power lines. In recent years, this has led to concerns about people becoming ill. This was not expected when power lines were built.

Power lines give off signals a bit similar to radio signals. In a few small areas, there have been reports of a higher level of a fatal illness called leukaemia (cancer of the blood) in people who live near power lines.

There is no definite evidence that living near power lines is dangerous. Scientists are trying to answer this question. If they find that there is a problem then the solution will be to move the cables or to move the people. In either case, it will have a big effect on the way people live.

Similar concerns have been expressed about mobile phones and mobile phone masts. The use of mobile phones has had a big impact on the way people live. If we find out there is a danger then the solution to the problem will probably produce another big change in the way people live.

Question 6 _____

Hydro-electric dams do not pollute but they need a large area of flooded land.

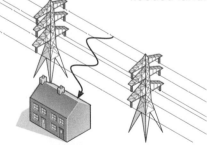

Power lines give out very low frequency, very long wavelength signals.

Zap your brain with a mobile phone!

It's good to talk.

7I.1

1 What do we need energy for?
Give some examples.

2 What type of energy does a moving object have?

3 What type of energy does a kettle produce?

4 What energy transfer takes place in an electric fire?

5 What do we call something we burn to get energy?

6 Give <u>two</u> examples of fuels being used.

7I.2

1 Name the <u>three</u> main fuels used in power stations.

2 Where did the energy in fossil fuels come from originally?

3 What does 'non-renewable' mean?

4 Give <u>two</u> reasons why it is important to find alternatives to fossil fuels.

5 Give <u>one</u> method of saving fossil fuels.

7I.3

1 What does <u>renewable</u> mean?

2 Give <u>one</u> example of a renewable type of energy.

3 Where do the tides get their energy from?

4 What is the name for the energy stored in plants?

5 Give <u>one</u> disadvantage of wind energy.

6 What causes wave energy?

7 Where does geothermal energy come from?

7I.4

1 What do animals get their energy for living from?
2 What is energy measured in?
3 How many joules are there in a kilojoule?
4 Why does exercise help keep weight down?
5 Who would need the most food – a PE teacher or a computer programmer?
   Give <u>one</u> reason for your answer.
6 Where does the energy in food come from originally?

7I.HSW

1 Imagine that some wind turbines are going to be put up near where you live.
   Write a letter expressing your view about the plan, as if you were going to send it to your local MP.
2 If all cars were converted to run on hydrogen as described, list the changes that you think would take place in people's lives.
3 For each of the problems in the table, say whether it is a technological problem, an ethical and moral problem, or a mixture of the two.
4 What do you think of the possible solutions in the table?
5 Find out what effect the Three Gorges Dam project in China is having on the people and wildlife in the area.
6 How would you react if you found out that using a mobile phone was slightly dangerous? Describe any changes in your lifestyle that would happen if you decided to use one less or even not at all.

Making a circuit

Electricity will only flow when a **circuit** is complete.
These diagrams show four attempts at making a **bulb** light up.
Only one will work.

switch

There is no source of
energy to make the
electricity flow, so the bulb
will not light up.

There is a gap. It is not
a complete circuit, so
the electricity cannot
flow around.

This circuit is connected
using wood. Wood does not
let electricity flow through it.
Wood is not a conductor.

copper wires

This is a complete circuit.
Electricity can flow and
the bulb will light up.

Using a switch

We use a **switch** to stop the current in a circuit.

When the switch is open, the circuit is not complete.
Electricity cannot flow.

Look at the diagram of the torch. When the switch is closed:

- there is a complete circuit;
- the bulb lights up.

When the switch is open:

- the circuit is not complete;
- the bulb is off.

You can <u>break</u> the circuit with a switch.
No electricity then flows.

When the circuit is complete,
electricity flows through the
switch and the bulb.

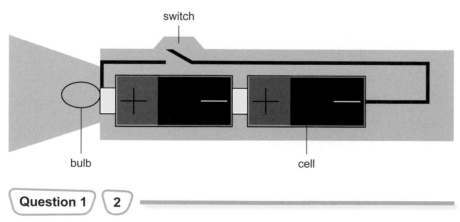

switch

bulb

cell

Question 1 / 2

Drawing a circuit

We use symbols to represent things in circuits.

These are used to draw circuits.

When you draw a circuit using symbols like this, it is called a **circuit diagram**.

Component	Symbol
cell	
connection	
open switch	
closed switch	
bulb	

Some common symbols.

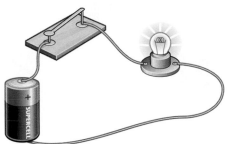

This is what a circuit looks like.

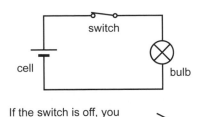

If the switch is off, you use the symbol for the open switch like this.

This is how you can draw it.

Question 3   4

If you connect a cell to two bulbs, you can make the electricity flow through each bulb in turn.

The drawing shows what the circuit looks like.

The circuit diagram is shown below the drawing.

Sometimes you use more than one cell in a circuit. Two or more cells joined together are called a battery.

This is confusing because many people use the word 'battery' to mean a single cell.

A battery has its own symbol.

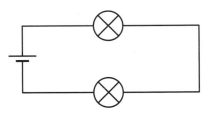

A current flows through one bulb and then through the other.

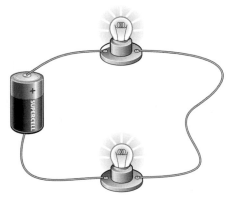

You can use a cell to get an electric current that is safe for experiments.

Two (or more) cells joined together make a battery.

This is the symbol for a battery.

Question 5   6

You should already know | Outcomes | Keywords

The things used in an electric circuit are called **components**. Bulbs and batteries are examples of components.

In a **series** circuit, all components are connected in one loop. This diagram shows a circuit with two bulbs in series.

When an electric current flows around a series circuit, there is only one path for it to follow. So it has to flow through all of the components.

The current flow is shown by arrows:

- from the positive side of the power supply
- around the circuit
- back to the negative side of the power supply.

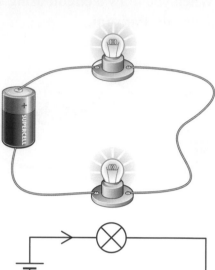

We measure the electric current with an **ammeter**. An ammeter tells us the value of the current in **amperes** (amps or 'A' for short).

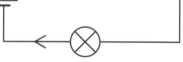 This is the symbol for an ammeter.

Two bulbs in a series circuit.

The diagram on the right shows how the ammeter should be connected.

The ammeter in the diagram is showing a reading of 0.15 amps, which is written as 0.15 A.

The box below shows where an ammeter can be put in this series circuit.

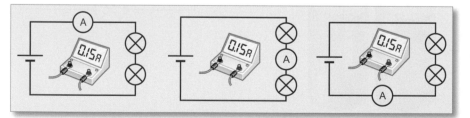

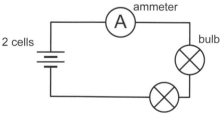

2 cells / ammeter / bulb

All of the ammeters show the same reading. The electric current is the same all the way round a series circuit. The current does not get used up. It stays the same as it goes through each bulb.

Question 1 | 2

Changing the current

Dimmer switches change the brightness of lights.

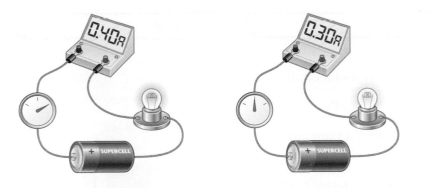

It is harder for the current to flow through some materials. We say that these materials have a high **resistance**. The current is smaller in a circuit with a high resistance The current is larger in a circuit with a low resistance.

This is the symbol for a resistor.

A variable resistor is used to change the resistance in a circuit. Variable resistors often have a control knob to change the size of the resistance.

This is the symbol for a variable resistor.

Volume controls are made from variable resistors.

A dimmer switch uses a variable resistor.

As you turn the dimmer switch, you change the resistance.

- Increasing the resistance makes the current smaller, which makes the bulb dimmer.
- Decreasing the resistance makes the current bigger, which makes the bulb brighter.

Adding bulbs to a circuit increases the total resistance of the circuit.

This means the current decreases.

The bulbs become less bright as the current falls.

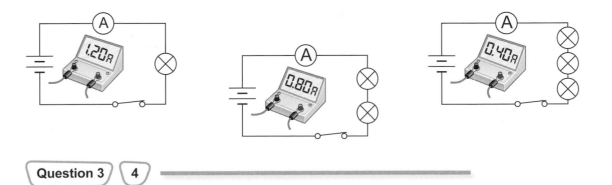

Question 3 4

Cells or batteries make an electric current flow round a circuit.

In this torch, the electric current is pushed by two **cells**.

Remember that two or more cells connected together are called a **battery**.

The strength of a cell is shown by a number with a letter V after it. This is called the voltage of the cell.

If you look on an AA cell you will see the voltage written as 1.5 V. The V stands for volts.

You can join cells together to make a larger voltage.

When cells are joined together they make groups of cells. These are called batteries.

The diagram shows cells joined together to make a 3 V battery and a 4.5 V battery.

Sometimes all the cells are wrapped inside the same case so you cannot see them. This is how the 9 V battery in the diagram is made.

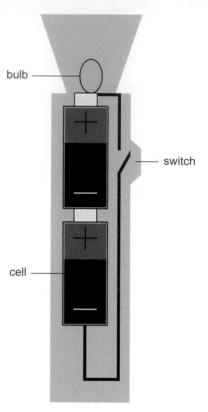

A 1.5 V cell.

Two 1.5 V cells make a 3.0 V battery.

Three 1.5 V cells make a 4.5 V battery.

A 9 V battery has six cells hidden inside the case.

Question 1 / 2 / 3

Inside a cell

A cell is made of chemicals. When a cell is in a complete circuit, the chemicals react and make the current flow.

There are lots of combinations of chemicals that will make cells. Some are better than others.

The top diagram shows three cells made from copper and zinc.

The lower diagram shows the chemicals inside a typical torch battery you can buy in a supermarket.

Inside a circuit

The flow of electric current around a circuit is like the flow of water around a system of pipes.

The cell or battery is like the pump.

An ammeter in the electrical circuit is like a paddle wheel that turns and tells you how fast the water flows in the pipes.

An ammeter measures the flow of an electric current in amperes.

The table compares the electrical circuit to the water circuit.

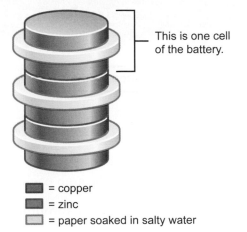

This is one cell of the battery.

■ = copper
■ = zinc
☐ = paper soaked in salty water

Alessandro de Volta (1745–1827) made the first battery in about 1800.

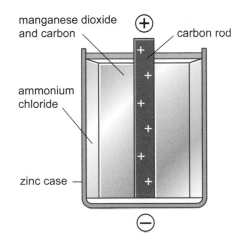

Cross section of a typical modern cell.

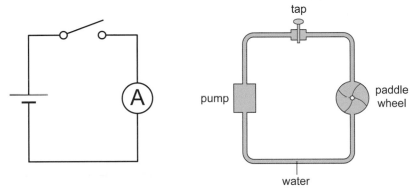

Electric current		Water current	
Object	Job	Object	Job
battery	pushes the current around the circuit	pump	pushes the water through the pipes
current	flows around the circuit	water	flows around the pipes
ammeter	shows how fast the current flows around the circuit	paddle wheel	shows how fast the water flows around the pipes
switch	breaks the circuit and the flow of current	tap	stops the flow of water

Comparing an electrical circuit to a water circuit.

Question 4 5

You should already know | Outcomes | Keywords

In a series circuit, there is one route for the current around the circuit.

The current flows through each bulb in turn.

The current is the same through each bulb.

The other main type of circuit is called a **parallel** circuit.

In a parallel circuit, each bulb has its own connection to the cell.

The current from the cell can split. Some current goes through one bulb and the rest goes through the other.

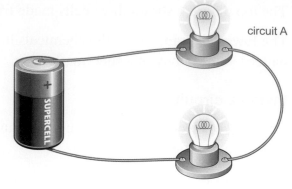

circuit A

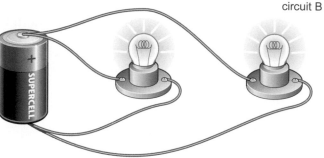

circuit B

In circuit B, each bulb is connected <u>separately</u> to the cell. We say that they are connected in parallel.

This circuit diagram shows two bulbs in a parallel circuit.

The electric current leaves the battery.

The current splits up at junction A:

- some current goes through bulb 1;
- some current goes through bulb 2.

When the current reaches junction B, it joins back together again.

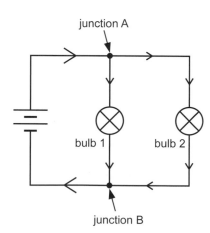

Question 1 | 2

What if a bulb breaks?

If a bulb breaks in a series circuit, it stops the current flowing.

The broken bulb is like a switch.

When it is broken there is not a complete circuit.

All the other bulbs in the circuit go off.

The filament of a bulb gives out light when a current flows through it.

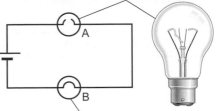

This bulb has a broken filament ...

A

B

... so this bulb doesn't light either.

Question 3

In a parallel circuit, one bulb can break and the other bulbs stay on.

This is because each bulb has its own connection to the cell.

Sometimes a series circuit is best.

Sometimes a parallel circuit is best.

House lights are connected in parallel. The parallel circuit lets you switch each light on or off on its own. This is what you want for the lights in a house.

Christmas tree lights are connected in series.

The series circuit can be safer because:

- the current in the circuit is smaller;
- you do not need as much wire to connect the bulbs.

Series circuit	Parallel circuit
if one bulb blows, all the bulbs go out	if one bulb blows, it does not affect the others
one switch operates all of the bulbs	each bulb can be turned on or off with its own switch
the power supply voltage is shared between the bulbs	each bulb gets the full power supply voltage
the current from the power supply is low	the current from the power supply is high

Comparing series and parallel circuits.

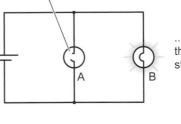

The filament of this bulb is broken...

...but this bulb stays on.

A   B

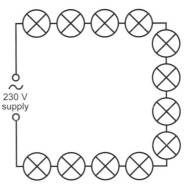

230 V supply

Tree lights in series.

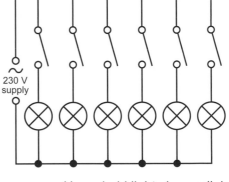

230 V supply

Household lights in parallel.

Question 4 **5**

Check your progress

You should already know   Outcomes   Keywords

Electricity is very useful but it can also be very dangerous.

Mains electricity is very dangerous. It uses a higher voltage than batteries.

Here are some reminders of things you must never do.

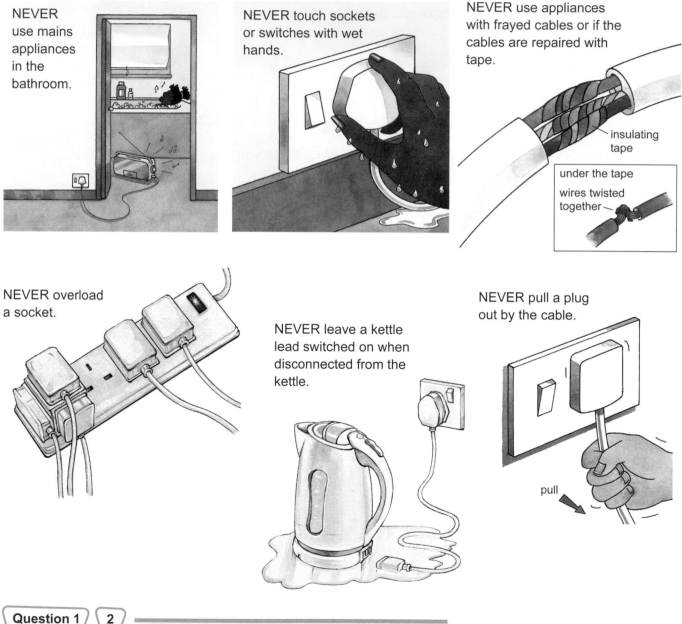

NEVER use mains appliances in the bathroom.

NEVER touch sockets or switches with wet hands.

NEVER use appliances with frayed cables or if the cables are repaired with tape.

insulating tape

under the tape

wires twisted together

NEVER overload a socket.

NEVER leave a kettle lead switched on when disconnected from the kettle.

NEVER pull a plug out by the cable.

pull

Question 1   2

Fuses

A large electric current can be very dangerous. It can cause a fire.

A **fuse** is used in a circuit to stop the current getting too big.

This is the circuit symbol for a fuse.

A fuse has a piece of wire inside it called fuse wire. If the current gets too big, the fuse wire gets hot and melts. When the fuse wire melts:

- the circuit is broken;
- the current stops flowing.

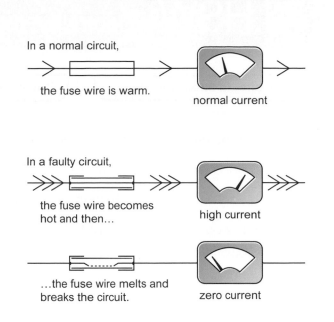

In a normal circuit, the fuse wire is warm.

normal current

In a faulty circuit, the fuse wire becomes hot and then...

high current

...the fuse wire melts and breaks the circuit.

zero current

Question 3 **4**

Mains plugs have three pins, called terminals. If you look inside a mains plug, there are three different colours of wire.

- The blue wire goes to the neutral terminal.
- The green-and-yellow wire goes to the earth terminal.
- The brown wire goes to the live terminal.

The live terminal is the one to which the fuse is connected.

The current stops if the fuse blows.

Fuses are made to melt at different current sizes.

The fuse in the plug diagram will melt when the current is 5A.

We say it has a 'rating' or 'size' of 5A.

Different things use different sizes of fuse.

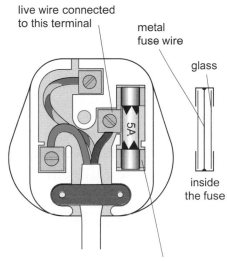

live wire connected to this terminal

metal fuse wire

glass

5A

inside the fuse

live pin in here

Household appliance	Typical fuse size
kettle	13 A
reading lamp	3 A
hairdryer	5 A
CD player	3 A
computer	3 A

Some typical fuse sizes.

Review your work

Question 5 **6**

Summary ➡

You should already know   Outcomes   Keywords

Using electric currents has transformed the way people live.

The first good electric light bulb was invented in 1879.

In 1900, very few homes in Britain used electricity for lighting.

In 2000, it would have been hard to find a home that did not have electric lights.

Now, we use electricity for many more things than lighting. We use it to make hundreds of different things work, like TV, kettles MP3 players and even electric toothbrushes.

We use electricity for communication and information transfer in television, telephones, the Internet and computing. These are only a few examples.

Electricity can kill. It is also quite difficult to make safely on a large scale.

There are some problems to solve with electricity.

Some are practical problems.

- How can we make enough electricity to meet the demand?
- How can we get the electricity from one place to another safely?
- How can people use electricity in their homes and stay safe?

Solving these problems is not only a matter of science. It involves **moral and ethical questions**. This is because different solutions have different effects on how people live and on the environment.

- Power stations contribute to global warming. Should we build more of them just because people want to use electricity or should we limit their use of it?
- Do power lines near homes make people ill?
- Does it matter if people electrocute themselves by being careless? Is it their own fault or should the design engineers make it impossible to happen by accident?

Using science has ethical and moral implications.

Electric lights like these have only been in common use for the past 70 years.

Large power stations produce electricity and cables carry the electricity all over the country.

Applying science to solve these problems is called **technology** or **engineering**.

Question 1   2   3

Assessing the risk

When you do an experiment in science, you must always assess the risks. This means thinking about all the things that could harm people or equipment. These are called **hazards**. You then work out what to do about each hazard with questions like

- Can I get the same result a different way with less hazard?
- How do I do this in a way that reduces the hazard?

In electricity experiments at school, the answers to these questions will be things like:

- use a battery or low voltage power supply for the experiment, not the mains;
- check that the circuit is connected correctly before it is turned on.

In the home and around the country, it is not as simple as that. Scientists and engineers need to answer questions like these.

- How far away from the houses must the power lines be?
- How high up should the power lines be?
- Should people be allowed to fit their own plugs and fuses?
- What size of voltage should we supply to people's homes?

In Europe, the voltage in homes is between 220 V and 240 V.

In North America and the Caribbean, it is 110 V.

The lower voltage is much safer. It is less likely to give a fatal shock if someone touches a bare wire. However, a lower voltage needs a higher current. This increases the risk of electricity causing fire.

Whether you supply electricity at 240 V or 110 V is about the balance between the risk of shocks and the risk of fire.

This engineer has assessed the risk. The strap from his wrist reduces the hazard of a spark from his body damaging the computer chips.

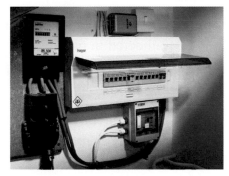

This fuse box has been designed to reduce hazards. It uses switches that can be reset. The user cannot touch any part carrying electricity.

A 13A plug from the UK, designed for maximum safety for the user.

Supply voltage	Reducing the risk	Disadvantages
110 V	Use thick wires so the high currents do not get them too hot.	Thick wires are a lot more expensive than thin ones.
240 V	Use well designed plugs and appliances so that people cannot get shocks	Safer designs adds to the cost of appliances.

Working out the balance between the risk of fire and the risk of fatal shock involves moral and ethical decisions and affects the way people live.

Question 4   5   6

7J.1

1 What type of circuit must you have for electricity to flow?

2 Why does opening a switch turn off a bulb?

3 Draw a simple circuit diagram with <u>two</u> bulbs and <u>one</u> cell.

4 What is the circuit symbol for a cell?

5 What is the name for two or more cells connected together?

6 What is the difference between a cell and a battery?

7J.2

1 What is the name for a circuit in which all of the components are connected in one loop?

2 What is used to measure the size of an electric current?

3 How does resistance affect the electric current in the circuit?

4 What happens to the brightness of a bulb in a series circuit when the resistance is made larger?

7J.3

1 What does the voltage of a cell tell you?

2 What is the difference between a cell and a battery?

3 How must one cell be connected to another in a battery?

4 If you compare an electric circuit to the flow of water in pipes, what does the battery compare to?

5 If you compare an electric circuit to the flow of water in pipes, what does the ammeter compare to?

7J.4

1   What is the name for a circuit in which each bulb has its own connection to the battery?

2   What does the current from the battery do when it meets a junction in a parallel circuit?

3   What happens to other bulbs in a series circuit if one bulb breaks? Give <u>one</u> reason for your answer.

4   Give <u>one</u> example of a situation where lights are connected in series.

5   Explain why it is better to wire house lights in parallel.

7J.5

1   How does the voltage in mains electricity compare with the voltage from batteries?

2   Give <u>three</u> safety rules for electricity in the home.

3   What is the job of a fuse in a plug?

4   What happens inside a fuse when it blows?

5   What are the <u>three</u> different colours of wire inside a mains plug and where do they go?

6   What will happen if you try to put a 6A current through a 5A fuse?

7J.HSW

1   Research the history of the electric light bulb (e.g. on the Internet).

2   List all the things you use in a day that need electricity. Write a short account of how you would manage without them. Find out how the use of electricity has changed peoples lives in the recent past.

3   Why is there a moral and ethical question about building a power line near to someone's house?

4   What problems still might happen with power lines even though they are put out of people's reach?

5   Most appliances come with a fitted plug so that people do not have to fit their own. This makes them a bit more expensive. Do you think this is a good thing or a bad thing? Justify your answer.

6   What are the advantages and disadvantages of the voltage levels used in different countries?

7K.1 About forces (HSW)

What do forces do?

Forces are all **pushes** or **pulls**. You can show them with an arrow. A **force** can:

- start something start moving;
- speed things up;
- slow things down;
- make something change its direction.

pull

The drawer moves in the same direction as you pull it.

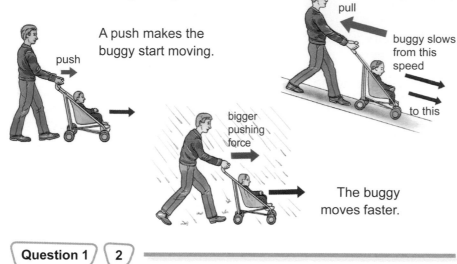

A push makes the buggy start moving.

push

A force in the opposite direction slows the buggy down.

pull

buggy slows from this speed

to this

bigger pushing force

The buggy moves faster.

The force from the player's head changes the direction of the ball.

Question 1 2 ──────────────

Two forces can cancel each other out. They must act in opposite directions to do this. This is what happens in a tug of war or when you hold up a weight. We call them **balanced forces**.

If something is still and the forces are balanced then it stays still. Things only speed up, slow down or change direction when the forces are not balanced.

equal and opposite forces balance out

Balanced forces.

lifting force of arm muscles

weight of dumb-bell

Question 3 ──────────────

Forces can be balanced when things are moving.

If something is moving and the forces are balanced then it does not speed up or slow down. It keeps moving at a steady speed.

This is what happens to a parachutist.

- The drag force of the air balances the force down.
- They fall at a steady speed.
- The speed of fall is slow enough for them to hit the ground safely.

A similar thing happens when someone rides a bike.

- The cyclist moves through the air.
- The air drags on the cyclist.
- The drag from the air balances the force pushing the cyclist forwards.
- The forces are balanced so the cyclist goes at a steady speed.

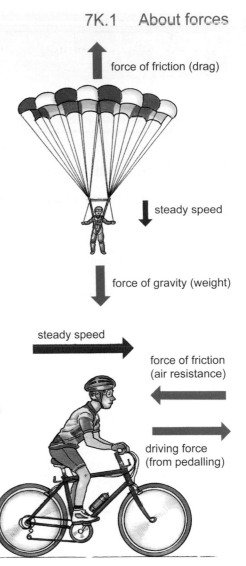

(Question 4) (5) ───────────────

Measuring forces

You measure forces in **newtons**.

Situation	Approximate force in newtons
pull of the Earth on a kilogram of sugar	10
weight of a 20 stone sumo wrestler	1 300
force on a racing car speeding up from 0 mph to 60 mph in 5 seconds	40 000

One newton is the size of force you need to lift a small apple. You need about 5 N to pick up a cup of tea.

You measure the size of a force with a newtonmeter. A newtonmeter has a spring inside it. Different forces stretch the spring by different amounts.

To measure large forces, you use a newtonmeter with a spring made of thick wire.

To measure small forces, you use a newtonmeter with a spring made of thin wire.

(Question 6) ───────────────

You should already know

Outcomes

Keywords

The Earth pulls things towards it

When something is dropped it falls towards the centre of the Earth. The force that pulls it down is called **weight**. The arrows in this diagram show the direction of this force on objects at different places around the Earth.

Weight is a force that happens whether or not the Earth and the object touch each other. You measure the weight of something when you hang it on a newtonmeter. The diagram shows the weight of some typical objects in newtons.

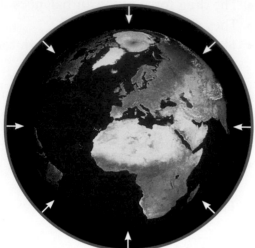

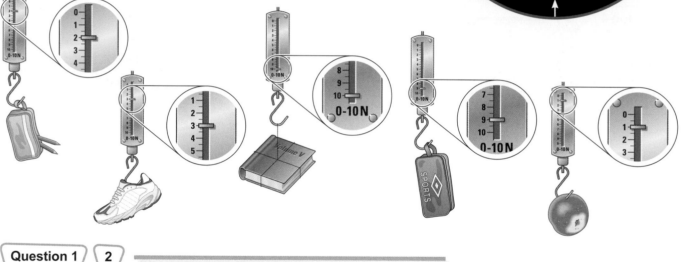

Question 1 / 2

What is gravity?

The weight of something is caused by **gravity**. Gravity is a force of attraction between all objects. The force of gravity is very weak.

You only notice it when one of the objects is very heavy, like the Earth.

The force of gravity between two apples is too small to notice. The force between an apple and the Earth is obvious.

If you let go of an apple, the Earth's gravity will make it fall down.

The force of gravity between two small objects is too small to notice.

The Earth has a very big mass. So there is a large force of gravity between the Earth and other objects.

Earth

Gravity on the Moon is less than it is on the Earth because the Moon is smaller than the Earth.

Weight and mass

Mass tells you how much stuff something is made of.

Mass is measured in kilograms.

In science, the word 'weight' always refers to a force. Weight is the pull of gravity on something.

The Earth pulls a 1 kilogram bag of sugar with a force of about 10 N.

The weight of the sugar is 10 newtons.

Object	Mass (g)	Mass (kg)	Weight (N)
DVD in case	100	0.1	1
classical guitar	1 400	1.4	14
litre bottle of squash	1 000	1	10
11 stone person	69 300	69.3	693

The weights and masses of some things on the Earth.

The Earth's gravity is about six times bigger than the Moon's.

 **Question 3** **4**

The weight of something is usually balanced by another force in the everyday world. The diagrams show some examples.

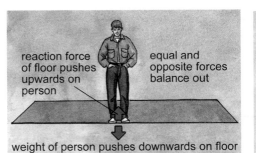

reaction force of floor pushes upwards on person

equal and opposite forces balance out

weight of person pushes downwards on floor

People don't fall through floors.

The weight of the book is balanced by a push from the table.

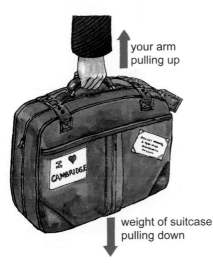

your arm pulling up

weight of suitcase pulling down

The two forces balance, so the suitcase stays still.

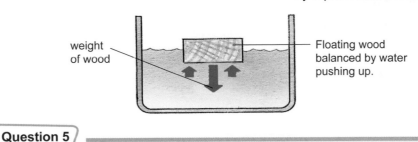

weight of wood

Floating wood balanced by water pushing up.

Question 5

Check your progress

7K.3 Friction

Friction is a force you get when two things try to move past each other.

It is an important force.

You could not walk without friction.

When you walk, you push your foot backwards. The friction force between your foot and the floor moves you forwards.

If you try the same thing off a skateboard, the skateboard moves back. There is no push from it to make you go forwards.

The wheels of the skateboard reduce the friction to a very low level.

Friction happens when things try to move past each other.

Look at the pictures of Eric and Sonja pushing the box.

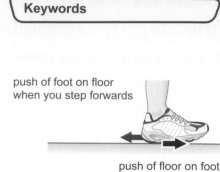

push of foot on floor when you step forwards

push of floor on foot moves you forwards

Your foot does not slide.

push of foot when you step forwards

The board moves back.

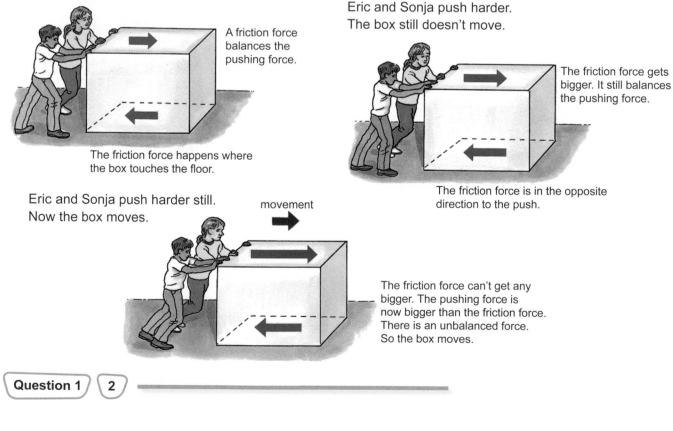

Eric and Sonja push the box.
It doesn't move.

A friction force balances the pushing force.

The friction force happens where the box touches the floor.

Eric and Sonja push harder.
The box still doesn't move.

The friction force gets bigger. It still balances the pushing force.

The friction force is in the opposite direction to the push.

Eric and Sonja push harder still.
Now the box moves.

movement

The friction force can't get any bigger. The pushing force is now bigger than the friction force. There is an unbalanced force. So the box moves.

Question 1 ⟩ 2 ⟩

Reducing friction

Friction can be a problem. You can reduce friction in three ways:

- make the surfaces smooth;
- put a **lubricant** like oil on them;
- make the moving parts so that they roll rather than slide.

Rollers reduce friction. This idea is used in the hub of a wheel. A wheel turns on sets of ball bearings. These reduce friction because they roll rather than slide. You can also reduce the friction by adding oil. We say that the oil lubricates the moving parts.

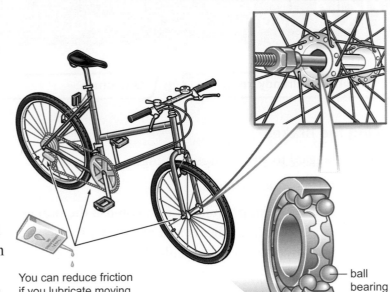

You can reduce friction if you lubricate moving parts with oil or grease.

Sliding surfaces must be smooth. If they are rough or rusty, there will be a lot of friction.

ball bearing

Ball bearings reduce friction because they roll rather than slide.

Question 3 4

Another friction force

The friction force when something slides through air or a liquid is called **drag**.

Drag can be very useful. If you want to slow down the fall of an object, you use a parachute. It provides a large drag force.

Some seeds have small wings or finc hairs that act like a parachutc. The drag of the air slows down the fall of the seeds and they can be spread out by the wind.

Seeds can travel a long way before they hit the ground. The new plant will not be competing with the original plant for food.

Drag makes it harder to speed things up.

Racing cars are made to make the drag as low as possible.

A car with a shape that moves through the air easily does not use as much petrol as a car with a lot of drag.

We say that the shape that goes through the air with less drag is more **streamlined**.

movement

The shape of this car gives it a lot of air resistance.

air resistance

The car has to push air out of the way.

Air can easily flow past the car...

We say that this car has a streamlined shape.

...so there is less air resistance.

Question 5 6

You should already know	Outcomes	Keywords

Using the brakes

Friction is used to stop things moving.

Brakes and tyres use friction.

When you want to stop a bike or car, you use the brakes. The brakes push on the wheels and produce a friction force. The friction force slows the wheels down.

Even if you have good brakes, you need a good grip on the road as well. If your tyres do not have a good grip or the road is too slippery, the friction force will be too small and you will skid.

This tyre is old and very worn. This tyre is brand new.

Did you know that a bald tyre actually grips a dry road better than a new tyre? But there is a problem when the road is even slightly damp or wet. On damp roads, the bald tyre will slip all over the place and cause accidents. There is a law against driving around with bald tyres.

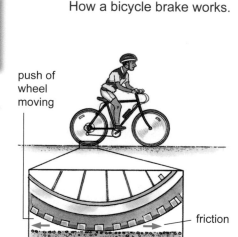

cable pulled

rubber block

pushes against wheel

How a bicycle brake works.

push of wheel moving

friction

The friction between a rubber tyre and a rough road surface moves the bike forwards.

Question 1	2

Speed and stopping

Speed tells you how far you go in a certain time.

30 miles per hour (mph) means you travel 30 miles in 1 hour.

20 km/h means you travel 20 kilometres in 1 hour.

The maximum speed that traffic is allowed to go at in built-up areas is 30 mph. That is the same as about 13 metres in a second (m/s).

	Speed in mph	Speed in km/h	Speed in m/s
Walking	4	6.4	1.8
Cycling	12	almost 20	5.4
Athlete running	22	36	10
Cheetah running	70	113	31.3
An athlete cannot run much further than 200 m at this speed. A cheetah can only keep its speed up for about 500 m.			

Some typical speeds in different units.

Question 3

The faster you go in a car, the longer it takes to stop.

The blue stripe shows the distance you travel while you are thinking about stopping. The **thinking distance** will be longer if a driver is

- tired
- affected by medicines, alcohol or drugs
- using a mobile phone.

The red stripe shows the distance you travel once you start to brake.

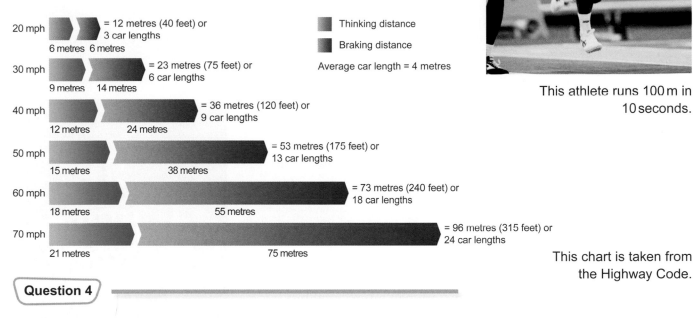

This athlete runs 100 m in 10 seconds.

This chart is taken from the Highway Code.

Question 4

Showing a journey on a graph

You can use a graph to draw a picture of a journey.
The graph in the diagram is called a distance–time graph.

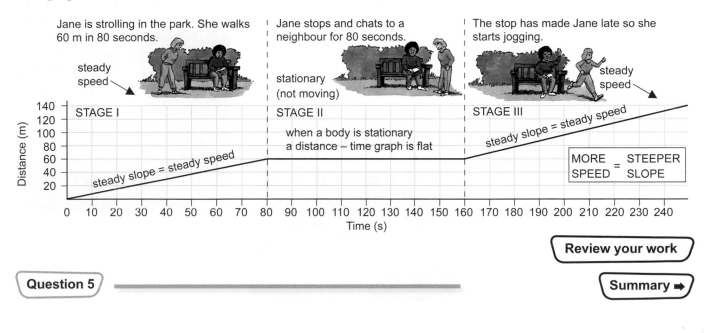

Review your work

Question 5

Summary ➡

You should already know

Outcomes

Keywords

Galileo and falling objects

Galileo was an Italian scientist. He lived from 1564 to 1642. He was one of the first scientists to use **experiments** and **mathematics** to answer questions and test ideas.

Until then, scientists tried to explain things by arguing about them. They tried to make everything fit in with the ideas of Greek and Arab thinkers from almost 2000 years earlier.

One old idea was that heavy objects fell faster than light objects. Galileo did experiments to test this idea. He proved that it was wrong with the observations from his experiments.

He was also very good at explaining things and he worked out a way of proving that the idea was wrong with words as well as with experiments.

He is supposed to have tested the idea by dropping a large cannon ball and a small metal ball at the same time from the top of the tower of Pisa. It is unlikely that he actually did this. We do know that he tested the idea in other ways with pendulums and by rolling a ball down a slope.

Question 1 2 ──────────

In science, we use evidence from observations and experiments.

Sometimes there is more than one way of approaching a scientific problem.

The Leaning Tower of Pisa.

Testing the ideas

Galileo thought that a feather falls more slowly than a coin because of the drag of air on the feather. He could not test this because he did not have a pump that could empty the air from a tube. He did describe how it might be done.

In 1969, Neil Armstrong (the first man to walk on the Moon) did a version of the experiment. He dropped a hammer and a feather side by side on the moon. The hammer and feather fell at exactly the same rate.

Galileo Galilei (known as Galileo) at the age of 42, in 1606.

Astronauts tested some of our ideas about motion on the Moon.

Isaac Newton and gravity

Galileo described how things fall but it was Isaac Newton (1642–1727) who explained why.

By the age of 24, he had worked out the idea of **gravity**. This explained why things fall and how moons go round planets and planets go round the Sun.

Newton tested his idea of gravity. He used the time the Moon took to go round the Earth and the distance from the Earth to the Moon to work out how fast an apple falls to the ground.

The result of his experiments did not match the calculation. He thought that his theory must be wrong.

About 6 years later, Newton got a better estimate for the distance from the Earth to the Moon. This time, the calculation for the fall of an apple worked out. It looked like Newton had got it right after all!

Newton's idea that gravity applied everywhere, on Earth and in the heavens, completely changed the way people thought and behaved. Newton's ideas and discoveries are one of the starting points for the **technological culture** we live in today.

> **Question 3** / **4**

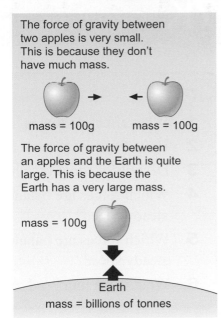

The force of gravity between two apples is very small. This is because they don't have much mass.

mass = 100g   mass = 100g

The force of gravity between an apples and the Earth is quite large. This is because the Earth has a very large mass.

mass = 100g

Earth
mass = billions of tonnes

Gravity is a force that attracts all masses to each other.

Woolsthorpe Manor, Lincolnshire. An ancestor of the apple tree here is supposed to have inspired Newton's ideas on gravity.

Light and gravity

In 1905, Albert Einstein produced a theory that explained gravity in a different way to Newton. Most scientists thought that the theory was wrong. One prediction was that gravity bends light very slightly. In 1919, astronomers measured the bending of light in a solar eclipse. This showed that Einstein was correct. Another result from this theory is the most famous formula in science: $E=mc^2$. This formula led to the discovery of nuclear power and **atomic weapons**. Einstein's theory has had a big impact on the politics of the world and the way we live today.

> The use of nuclear power and atomic weapons raise big moral and ethical questions about the use of science. Einstein warned people about this before atomic weapons or nuclear power had been made to work.

> **Question 5**

Technological culture
Things like air travel, road transport, anything that uses light (including lasers), accurate clocks and watches, anything to do with satellites (including television), and mobile phones can all be traced back to Isaac Newton in some way.

7K.1

1 What effect do forces have on objects?

2 How do you represent a force on a diagram?

3 Describe a situation where forces are balanced.

4 Which forces are balanced when a parachutist is falling at a steady speed?

5 Which forces are balanced when a cyclist is riding at a steady speed?

6 What is the unit used to measure force?

7K.2

1 What is the name for the pull of the Earth on something?

2 What is the weight of the book shown in the diagram?

3 What is the name for how much stuff something is made of?

4 What weight does a 1 kg mass have on Earth?

5 Explain why the weight of a person does not make them fall through the floor.

7K.3

1 What is the name for the force you get when two things try to move past each other?

2 In what direction does a friction force act when you try to push a box along a floor?

3 Give <u>three</u> things you can do to reduce friction.

4 Name <u>one</u> place where rollers are used to reduce friction.

5 What can affect the size of a drag force?

6 What is the advantage for a car if you can reduce the drag?

7K.4

1 How do brakes stop a car?

2 What can happen if the friction force between the road and the wheel is too small?

3 Which travels faster – an athlete or a cheetah?

4 What can affect a driver's thinking distance?

5 Which section of the graph shows Jane travelling fastest? How can you tell?

7K.HSW

1 Find out what other things Galileo is famous for as well as studying falling objects. How have any of these things affected the way people live?

2 If the Greek philosophers had been correct, what would Galileo have observed if he had done the experiment at the Tower of Pisa?

3 Why was the Moon a good place to test Galileo's idea that heavy and light objects fall together if there is no air resistance?

4 The University of Cambridge was closed for 2 years from 1665 because of a problem in London. This caused Newton to stay at Woolsthorpe Manor and do a lot of constructive thinking.
Find out what the problem in London was.
Which developments in science stop the same problem happening today?

5 The first use of atomic weapons was in Japan in 1945 at Hiroshima. The destruction was terrible. Countries like North Korea are trying to develop their own atomic weapons as this book is being written. The United States of America already has atomic weapons and is trying to stop other countries developing them.
Discuss what you think about countries developing atomic weapons.

Every day the Sun:

- rises in the **East**;
- moves across the sky during the day;
- sets in the **West**.

This is because the Earth spins round once every day.

The Earth spins in front of the Sun.

Earth   Sun

Imagine a giant stick through the centre of the Earth from the North Pole to the South Pole. The line of the stick is called the Earth's **axis**. The Earth spins around this axis.

- It turns every 24 hours.
- 24 hours is called a day.

The spin of the Earth explains why we get day and night.

- It is day for the part of the Earth's surface facing the Sun.
- It is night for the part of the Earth facing away from the Sun.

In the first picture below, the UK is facing the Sun and so it is daytime there.

Australia is facing away from the Sun and it is night time there.

India is just entering the dark side, so it is dusk.

12 hours later, in the second picture below, it is night time in the UK and daytime in Australia. In India it is getting light, so it is dawn.

The Earth spins around this axis.

N pole   sunlight

axis

S pole

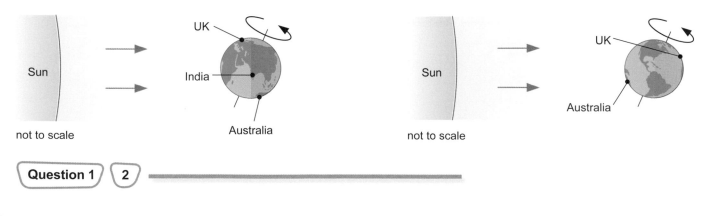

not to scale   Sun   UK   India   Australia   not to scale   Sun   UK   Australia

Question 1   2

The Earth travels around the Sun.

The path of the earth round the sun is called its **orbit**.
We say that the Earth orbits the Sun.

It takes the Earth 1 year to orbit the Sun.

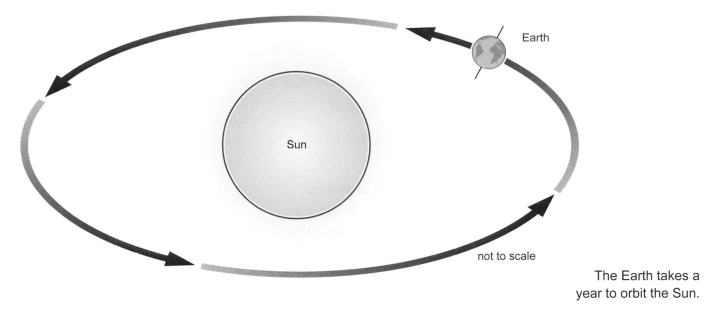

Earth

Sun

not to scale

The Earth takes a
year to orbit the Sun.

It takes the Earth 365¼ days to go once around the Sun.

Calendars only work in whole numbers of days. We say a year is
365 days long. This means that a year on the calendar is actually
one-quarter of a day short.

To make up the time, we add a day
to the end of February every 4 years.
This is called a leap year.

Here is a poem to remember this by.

Thirty days hath September, April, June and November.

All the rest have 31, except February alone,

Which has 28 days and 29 in a leap year.

2008 was a leap year. Here is the calendar for February in 2008.

Mon	Tue	Wed	Thu	Fri	Sat	Sun
				1	2	3
4	5	6	7	8	9	10
11	12	13	14	15	16	17
18	19	20	21	22	23	24
25	26	27	28	29		

Question 3 4 5 _____

You should already know | Outcomes | Keywords

As we go through a year in the UK, things change.

- It is warm in summer and cold in winter.
- The days are longer in summer than they are in winter.

These changes happen because the Earth's axis is **tilted**.

Different parts of the Earth are tilted towards the Sun or away from it during the year.

The top half of the Earth is called the northern **hemisphere**. The bottom half is called the southern hemisphere. When your hemisphere is tilted towards the Sun, you are in summer. When your hemisphere is tilted away from the Sun, you are in winter.

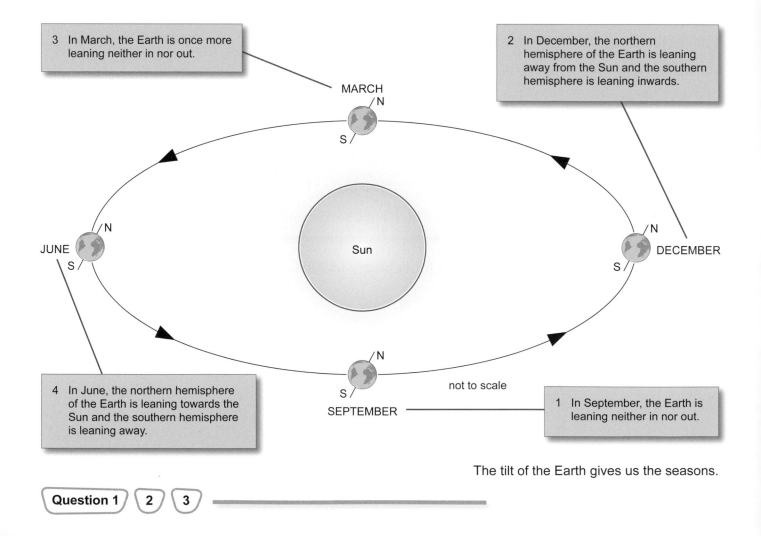

3 In March, the Earth is once more leaning neither in nor out.

2 In December, the northern hemisphere of the Earth is leaning away from the Sun and the southern hemisphere is leaning inwards.

4 In June, the northern hemisphere of the Earth is leaning towards the Sun and the southern hemisphere is leaning away.

1 In September, the Earth is leaning neither in nor out.

not to scale

The tilt of the Earth gives us the seasons.

Question 1 | 2 | 3

Why it is warmer in summer

The tilt of the Earth's axis and the curve of the Earth's surface make it warmer in summer in the UK.

In summer, the UK is tilted towards the Sun. This means that the rays of light from the Sun are more concentrated. They have more effect.

In winter, the UK is tilted away from the Sun. The light is spread over a larger area than it is in the summer. The Sun's rays are less concentrated and so the Earth's surface does not get so warm.

In summer, daytime lasts longer. The Sun's rays have longer to heat the surface. This helps to raise the temperature.

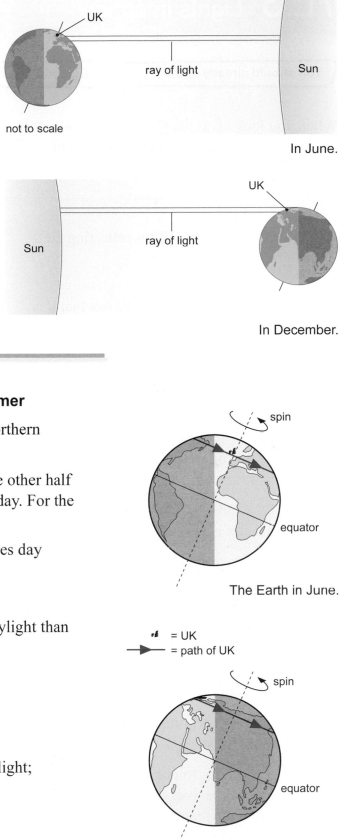

In June.

In December.

Question 4

Why we have more hours of daylight in summer

Summer days are longer than winter days in the northern hemisphere.

At any time, half of the Earth faces the Sun and the other half is hidden from it. For the half facing the Sun, it is day. For the hidden half, it is night.

The Earth's axis is at an angle to the line that divides day from night.

In June in the UK:

- the northern hemisphere spends more time in daylight than in darkness;
- the Sun is above the horizon for up to 16 hours;
- the Sun appears high up in the sky;
- The 21st of June is the longest day.

In December in the UK:

- the northern hemisphere spends less time in daylight;
- the Sun is above the horizon for about 8 hours;
- the Sun appears low down in the sky;
- The 21st of December is the shortest day.

Question 5 **6**

7L.3 Lights in space

You should already know   Outcomes   Keywords

When you look up at the sky on a clear night away from street lights, you can see lots of dots of light.

- Some are **stars**.
- Some are **planets**.
- Some are artificial **satellites** reflecting the sunlight.

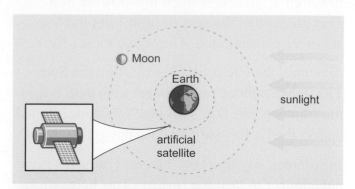

Moon

Earth

sunlight

artificial satellite

A star gives out its own light. We say that it is **luminous**. Stars are spread throughout the Universe.

The nearest star to the Earth is the Sun.

The stars seem to move slowly around the sky in circles.

You can see this on the photograph taken over several hours.

The stars all seem to move around a star called Polaris. This star is also known as 'the pole star'.

Each star appears to move around the pole star.

This happens because the Earth's axis points at Polaris and the Earth is spinning on its axis.

Stars are massive. Our Sun is over 100 times bigger than the Earth.

If the Sun was the size of a football then the Earth would be about the size of a peppercorn on the same scale.

Things to do with the Sun are said to be **solar**.

The group of planets going round the Sun are called the Solar System.

The next nearest star to our Solar System is a very long way away. It is over a quarter of a million times further away than the Sun is from us. The light from it takes 4 years to reach us.

Like the Sun and Moon, the stars seem to move across the sky. Only the pole star stays in the same place. This gives us further evidence that the Earth is spinning.

Solar System

It takes light 4 years to travel this distance.

Proxima Centauri

Question 1   2

Planets

There are nine planets orbiting the Sun.

Planets are giant lumps of rock or balls of gas.
They do not give out light but they can reflect it.

We can only see planets because they reflect the Sun's light.

Mercury, Venus, Mars and Jupiter can all be seen without
telescopes. They just look like stars in the sky.

The more distant planets (Saturn, Uranus, Neptune and
Pluto) are much harder to see because they are further away.
You need a telescope to look at these planets.

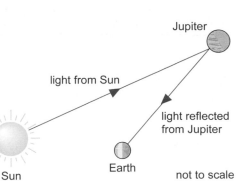

Question 3 / 4

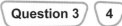

The Moon

The Moon orbits the Earth. It is not a planet.
It is called a satellite of the Earth.

The Moon does not give out its own light;
it reflects light from the Sun.

Things to do with the Moon are said to be **lunar**.

Phases of the Moon

Half of the Moon is in sunlight and half is in darkness. We can
only see the part of the Moon that faces us if it is reflecting light
from the Sun. The Moon does not give out any light of it own.

The part of the Moon that is facing us does not all reflect sunlight.
As the Moon moves round the Earth, the amount of the side we
see reflecting light varies.

The Moon takes 28 days to orbit the Earth. This is called a
lunar month.

When the light side of the Moon is completely facing us, we see a
Full Moon. It looks like a disc.

At the end of the lunar month, the side of the Moon that is in
shadow is facing us. We do not see the Moon at this point because
the side facing us is not reflecting any light from the Sun.

The stages that we see are known as the **phases** of the Moon.

The Moon.

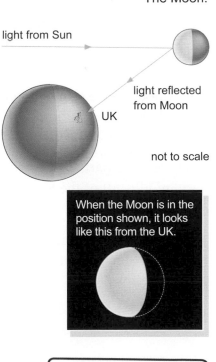

When the Moon is in the position shown, it looks like this from the UK.

Question 5 / 6

Check your progress

You must **never** look directly at the Sun even you're wearing sunglasses. The Sun is so bright that its light can permanently damage your eyes.

The Sun and the Moon look about the same size.

The Sun is actually 400 times bigger than the Moon. If the Sun was the size of a house, the Moon would be the size of a mouse.

The Sun is nearly 400 times further away from the Earth than the Moon is.

The difference in their sizes is cancelled out by the difference in their distances from the Earth. They appear to be the same size in the sky.

the setting Sun

the Moon in exactly the same direction at a different time

The Sun and the Moon look the same size.

Eclipses

Because the Moon appears to be the same size as the Sun, it can blot the Sun out if it gets into just the right position.

This can happen when the Moon passes between the Sun and the Earth. When this happens, it is called a **solar eclipse**.

The Moon casts a shadow on the surface of the Earth. Part of the Earth is dark, even though it is daytime!

There are two parts to the Moon's shadow. In the very middle, all of the Sun is blocked out. This is called a total eclipse.

There is also a part shadow where only some of the Sun is blocked out. People in this area see a **partial eclipse**.

x = total eclipse

not to scale

An eclipse of the Sun happens when the Earth is in the Moon's shadow.

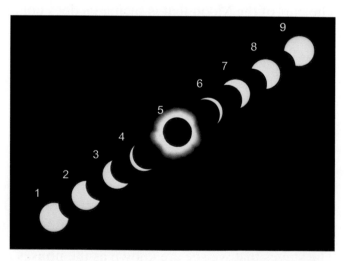

Nine photos of the stages of a total solar eclipse. Number 5 shows totality.

Question 1 / 2

The orbit of the Moon around the Earth is at a slight angle compared with the orbit of the Earth around the Sun.

This means that the Earth, Moon and Sun do not line up very often.

Solar eclipses do not happen very often over the same place on the Earth. Between 1724 and 1927, there were no total eclipses in the UK.

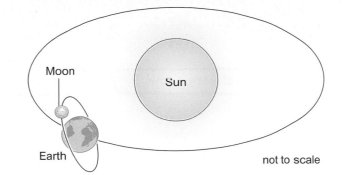

not to scale

Date	Notes
1st August 2008	partial eclipse
4th January 2011	partial eclipse in south-east England
20th March 2015	partial eclipse
11th August 2018	partial eclipse in the north of Scotland
23rd September 2090	total eclipse in Cornwall lasting 2 minutes and 10 seconds

The solar eclipses visible from the UK in this century.

Question 3

Lunar eclipses

The second type of eclipse we see from the Earth is called a **lunar eclipse**.

A lunar eclipse happens when the Moon has moved into the Earth's shadow.

The Moon does not completely disappear. The Earth's atmosphere bends some light from the Sun around to the Moon. This means that the Moon is lit up by a faint glow.

Look at the middle of the photograph. You can see that the Moon is a faint reddish orange colour, a bit like copper metal, when the total eclipse happens.

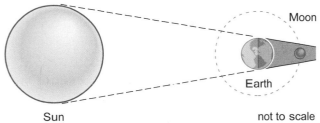

not to scale

An lunar eclipse happens when the Moon is in the Earth's shadow.

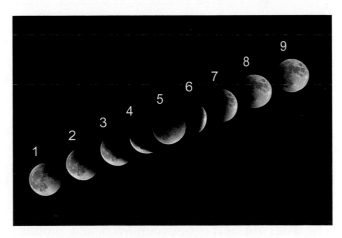

Nine photos of a total lunar eclipse.

Question 4   **5**

You should already know

Outcomes

Keywords

The Sun and planets together are called the **Solar System**.

The telescope was invented in about 1610.

Some planets can only be seen with a telescope so they were not discovered until after 1610.

Planet	Discovery date
Mercury, Venus, Mars, Jupiter	known since ancient times
Saturn	known since ancient times, but the rings were discovered by Galileo in 1610 with one of the first telescopes
Uranus	1781
Neptune	1846
Pluto	1930

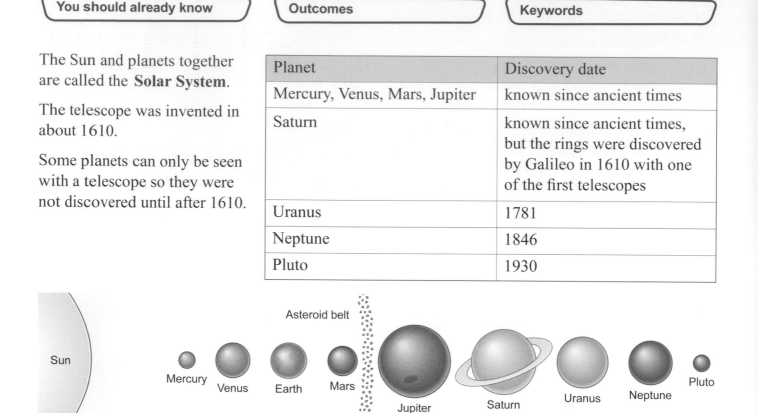

not to scale

The Solar System.

Here is a phrase to remember the order of the planets.
Each word starts with the same letter as the planet's name.

My	Very	Easy	Method	Just	Speeds	Up	Naming	Planets
Mercury	Venus	Earth	Mars	Jupiter	Saturn	Uranus	Neptune	Pluto

Question 1 **2**

Mercury, Venus, Earth and Mars have a surface that is made from rock. They are called the <u>rocky planets</u>.

Jupiter, Saturn, Uranus and Neptune are large balls of gas and are called the <u>gas giants</u>.

Pluto is very small and is made of rock and ice. It is sometimes called an <u>ice dwarf</u>.

The **asteroid belt** is between Mars and Jupiter. Asteroids are rocks that are not big enough to be planets. They might be from a planet that broke up a long time ago.

The surface of Mars.

How can you tell planets from stars?

If you look carefully at the same patch of sky every night for a few weeks, you can tell if there is a planet there.

The stars stay in fixed patterns but the planets gradually move about.

The word 'planet' means 'wanderer'. It comes from the idea that planets seem to wander about in the sky.

If you look at a planet with a powerful telescope, it will appear bigger.

If you look at a star, it is so far away that it just looks the same.

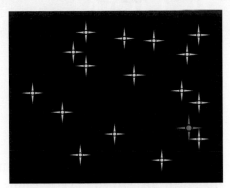

Part of the night sky.

Question 3   4

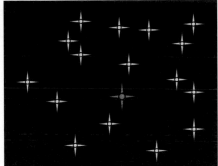

The <u>same</u> part of the night sky a few weeks later. All the <u>stars</u> are in the same places but the <u>planet</u> has moved.

Is there life on Mars or anywhere else?

Spacecraft have landed on Mars and put robots there to make observations and do experiments. These missions tell us that there are no large living things on Mars.

Robots have tested Martian soil for small living things like bacteria. If soil contains bacteria then the atmosphere above the soil is affected. Nothing has been found.

If there was life on Mars a long time ago then there might be fossils to show evidence of it. We find fossils in rocks on Earth from plants, animals and even bacteria that lived and died millions of years ago.

Scientists have not found any good evidence of fossils on Mars.

There are other stars in the Universe with planets going around them, but they are too far away to reach with spacecraft. It would take over 400 000 years for a spacecraft to reach the next nearest star if it went at 1000 km/h!

Scientists look for evidence for life outside our Solar System using signals like radio waves that we can detect. Nothing has been detected yet.

If you look at stars through a telescope, they still look exactly the same size. This is because they are so far away.

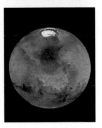

If you look at Mars through a telescope, it looks a lot bigger. This tells us that Mars isn't too far away from the Earth.

Question 5   6

Review your work

Summary ➡

You should already know | Outcomes | Keywords

Explaining what we see

Most people used to think the stars and planets moved around the earth. In 270 BC, Aristarchus suggested that the Earth moved around the Sun. His idea was rejected because:

- it didn't have human beings at the centre of the Universe;
- it did not explain why things did not fall off the Earth as it flew through space;
- people believed that the view of the stars would change as the Earth moved closer and further away, and this did not happen.

Copernicus suggested a similar idea in 1543. People rejected it for the same reasons.

In 1610, Galileo made a **telescope** and used it to look at the planets and stars. He worked out that the stars were a lot further away than people thought. This meant the view would not change if the Earth did go around the Sun. He also saw four moons going around Jupiter. He thought that this was how the Earth went around the Sun. He told everyone that Copernicus had had the right idea.

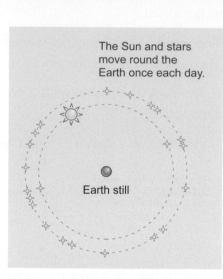

What people used to think happens.

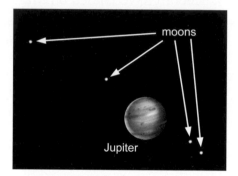

Galileo observed the planet Jupiter through his telescope. He saw at least four moons in orbit around it.

Question 1 | 2

Our view of the Universe today comes from the work of many people.

Name	Nationality	Dates	Contribution
Tycho Brahe	Danish	1546–1601	made thousands of accurate observations
Johannes Kepler	German	1571–1630	worked out laws about the way planets moved
Galileo	Italian	1564–1642	used arguments, experiments and observations to support the ideas of Copernicus
Isaac Newton	English	1642–1726	worked out the full answer and explained why it worked

Question 3

Improving the view

Newton did a lot of experiments on the behaviour of light. He made a much better telescope than Galileo had. His telescope used a curved mirror rather than a lens. The type of telescope he invented produces true colours.

This design of telescope is still used today to analyse the colour of light from stars.

Question 4

Air pollution makes telescope images hazy.

In 1990, a large telescope called the Hubble Space Telescope was put into space. You can find images from it on the Internet.

Space science has provided us with results that affect the way we live.

We use **satellites** for communications. Signals are transmitted from the Earth's surface to a satellite and then sent back down so they reach around the curved surface of the Earth.

This is useful for isolated communities. People in remote islands like the Maldives can get warnings of approaching tidal waves so that they can escape disaster.

Satellites are used for systems that tell you where you are on the Earth's surface. These global positioning system devices (GPS for short) are fitted to many cars and are used by taxis and ambulances.

Some satellites use telescopes to take pictures of the Earth's surface. The pictures are used in weather forecasting.

There are websites that show telescope photographs of the Earth's surface from space. The images are so good that you can tell if people have washing hanging on a line or not!

When we use and apply science like this, there are always **ethical questions**. Here are some examples.

- Are the advantages of communications and GPS systems worth the cost?
- Should we be spending billions of dollars on a telescope like Hubble just to get a clearer view of the stars?
- Is it right to spy on people from space?
- All these developments contribute to carbon emissions in some way and this contributes to global warming. Is that right?

Question 5 **6**

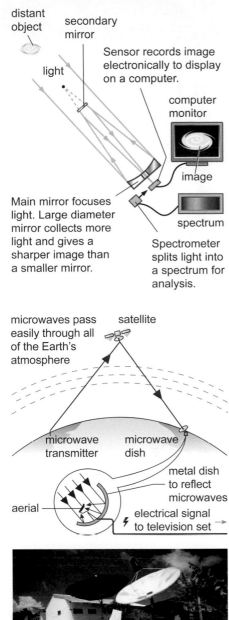

Satellite dish in the Maldives.

The creative application of science can bring about changes in the way people think and behave.

The use of scientific ideas has ethical and moral implications.

7L.1

1 How many hours are there in a day?

2 What is name for the line that the Earth spins around?

3 How long does it take the Earth to go round the Sun?

4 What is a leap year?

5 Which month has a different number of days in a leap year?

7L.2

1 Name <u>two</u> things that change as you go through the year.

2 What does 'tilted' mean?

3 Which part of the Earth spends more time nearer the Sun in June?

4 Give <u>two</u> reasons why it is warmer in summer in the northern hemisphere.

5 How does the length of a day in June in the UK compare with the length of a day in December?

6 How does the height of the Sun in the sky in December compare with the height of the Sun in the sky in June?

7L.3

1 Why do all the stars in the sky seem to move around Polaris?

2 What word is used to describe things to do with the Sun?

3 How many planets go round the Sun?

4 What is the difference between a planet and a star?

5 How long does it take the Moon to go round the Earth?

6 What do we call the changing appearance of the Moon?

7L.4

1   The Sun is a lot bigger than the Moon but it appears to be the same size. Why is that so?
2   What is the name for an eclipse of the Sun?
3   When is the next total eclipse of the Sun visible from the UK?
4   What is a lunar eclipse?
5   Which colour does the Moon go during a total lunar eclipse?

7L.5

1   What is meant by 'the Solar System'?
2   What is the name of the third planet from the Sun?
3   What is the difference between the material that makes up the Earth and the material that makes up Jupiter?
4   How can you tell the difference between a planet and a star by observing the sky?
5   What have scientists done to see if there might be life on Mars?
6   Why are spacecraft no use to find out if there is life outside our Solar System?

7L.HSW

1   Why did people think that Aristarchus and later Copernicus had the wrong idea?
2   What technological development helped Galileo work out that Copernicus had the right idea?
3   Find out what Tycho Brahe saw in 1572, why it was important and why he had a false nose made from silver and gold!
4   How was Newton's telescope better than Galileo's?
5   The Hubble space telescope is named after the astronomer Edwin Hubble. Research him on the Internet and find out what he is famous for.
6   What is your opinion of these four questions?

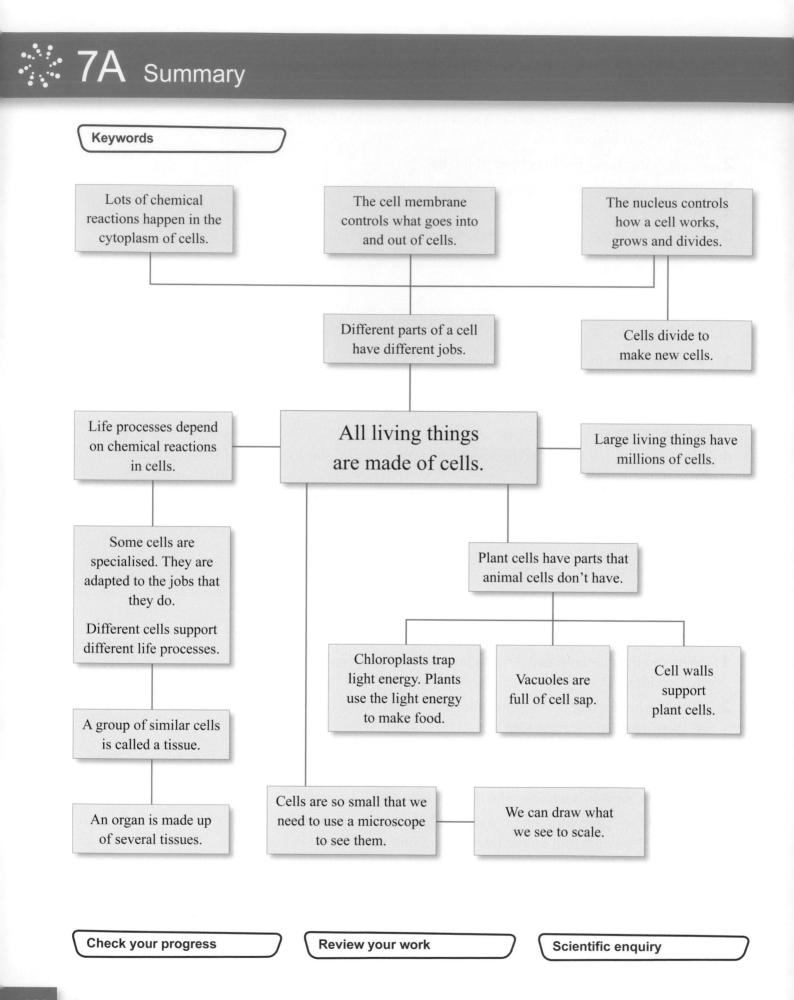

Keywords

Lots of chemical reactions happen in the cytoplasm of cells.

The cell membrane controls what goes into and out of cells.

The nucleus controls how a cell works, grows and divides.

Different parts of a cell have different jobs.

Cells divide to make new cells.

Life processes depend on chemical reactions in cells.

All living things are made of cells.

Large living things have millions of cells.

Some cells are specialised. They are adapted to the jobs that they do.

Different cells support different life processes.

Plant cells have parts that animal cells don't have.

A group of similar cells is called a tissue.

Chloroplasts trap light energy. Plants use the light energy to make food.

Vacuoles are full of cell sap.

Cell walls support plant cells.

An organ is made up of several tissues.

Cells are so small that we need to use a microscope to see them.

We can draw what we see to scale.

Check your progress   Review your work   Scientific enquiry

Key ideas

1 • Living things produce young of the same kind as themselves.
We say that they reproduce.

• Different creatures reproduce in different ways.

2 • In sexual reproduction, the nuclei of sex cells join, or fuse.
We call this fertilisation.

• In flowering plants, the sex cells are in the pollen grains and the ovules. In animals, the sex cells are sperm and egg cells. They are specialised to do their jobs.

• Sperm and egg nuclei contain inherited material from the parent that made them.

3 • Women have a monthly cycle controlled by hormones. We call it the menstrual cycle. As part of this cycle, an egg cell is released and menstruation happens about once a month.

• The menstrual cycle stops when a woman becomes pregnant.

4 • A fertilised egg cell divides and grows to form an embryo.
It is implanted in the uterus.

• When the embryo has grown all its main organs, we call it a fetus. The amniotic fluid cushions it. Substances pass between the fetus and mother through the placenta and umbilical cord.

5 • After it is born, mammary glands (breasts) produce milk for the baby.

• Human children are dependent on their parents and other adults for a long time.

6 • The time between childhood and adulthood is called adolescence. Hormones control the changes that take place during this time.

• We call the time of sexual maturity puberty. This is when eggs and sperm are first released.

Keywords

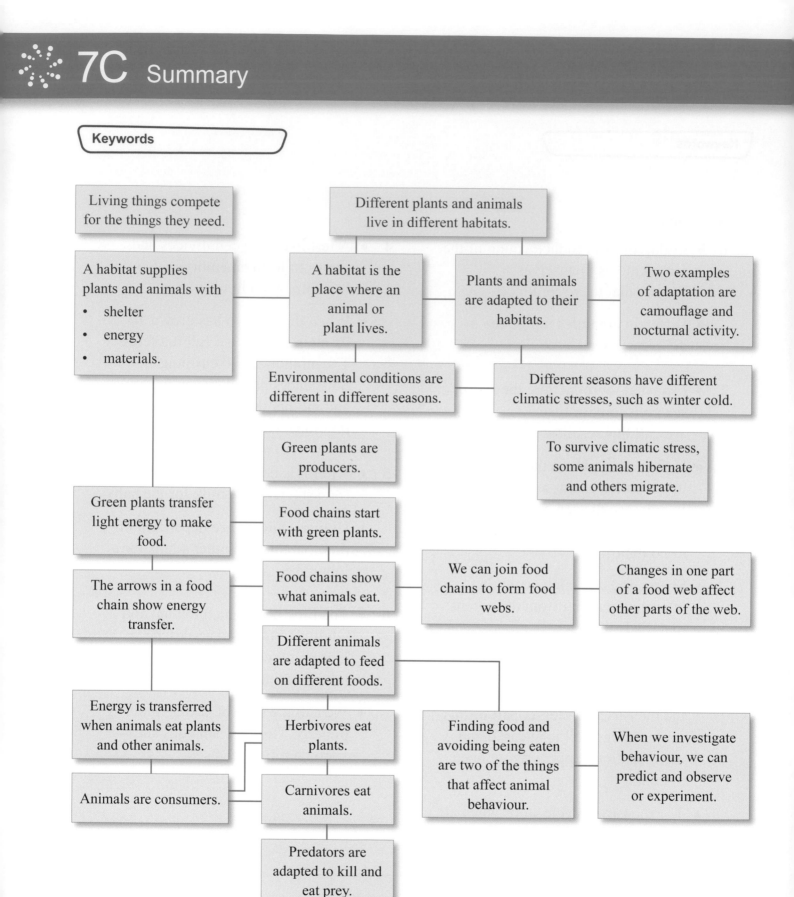

Living things compete for the things they need.

Different plants and animals live in different habitats.

A habitat supplies plants and animals with
- shelter
- energy
- materials.

A habitat is the place where an animal or plant lives.

Plants and animals are adapted to their habitats.

Two examples of adaptation are camouflage and nocturnal activity.

Environmental conditions are different in different seasons.

Different seasons have different climatic stresses, such as winter cold.

To survive climatic stress, some animals hibernate and others migrate.

Green plants are producers.

Green plants transfer light energy to make food.

Food chains start with green plants.

The arrows in a food chain show energy transfer.

Food chains show what animals eat.

We can join food chains to form food webs.

Changes in one part of a food web affect other parts of the web.

Different animals are adapted to feed on different foods.

Energy is transferred when animals eat plants and other animals.

Herbivores eat plants.

Finding food and avoiding being eaten are two of the things that affect animal behaviour.

When we investigate behaviour, we can predict and observe or experiment.

Animals are consumers.

Carnivores eat animals.

Predators are adapted to kill and eat prey.

Check your progress   Review your work   Scientific enquiry

Keywords

Key ideas

- A species is one kind of living thing.

- Members of a species
  — breed with each other
  — and produce fertile offspring.

- Individuals of the same species vary.

- Inherited variations pass from parents to offspring.

- Environmental variations do not pass from parents to offspring. They are caused by what happens to a plant or animal in its lifetime.

- Sorting things into groups is called classification. We put living things with the same characteristics in a group.

- We divide large groups into smaller groups.

- Scientists all over the world use the same classification system. This means that they all know which animals or plants they are writing about.

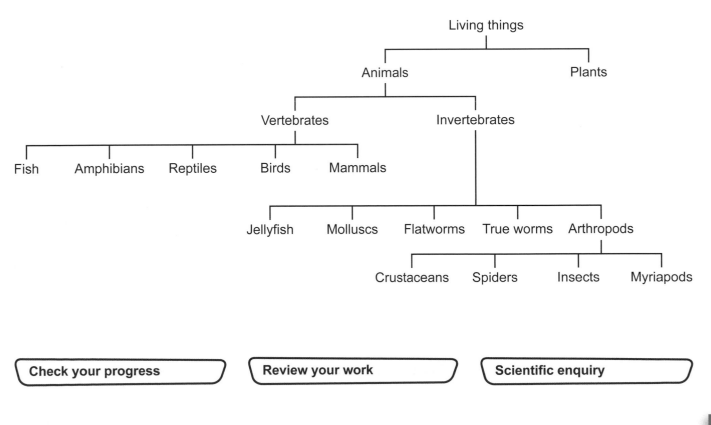

Check your progress   Review your work   Scientific enquiry

Keywords

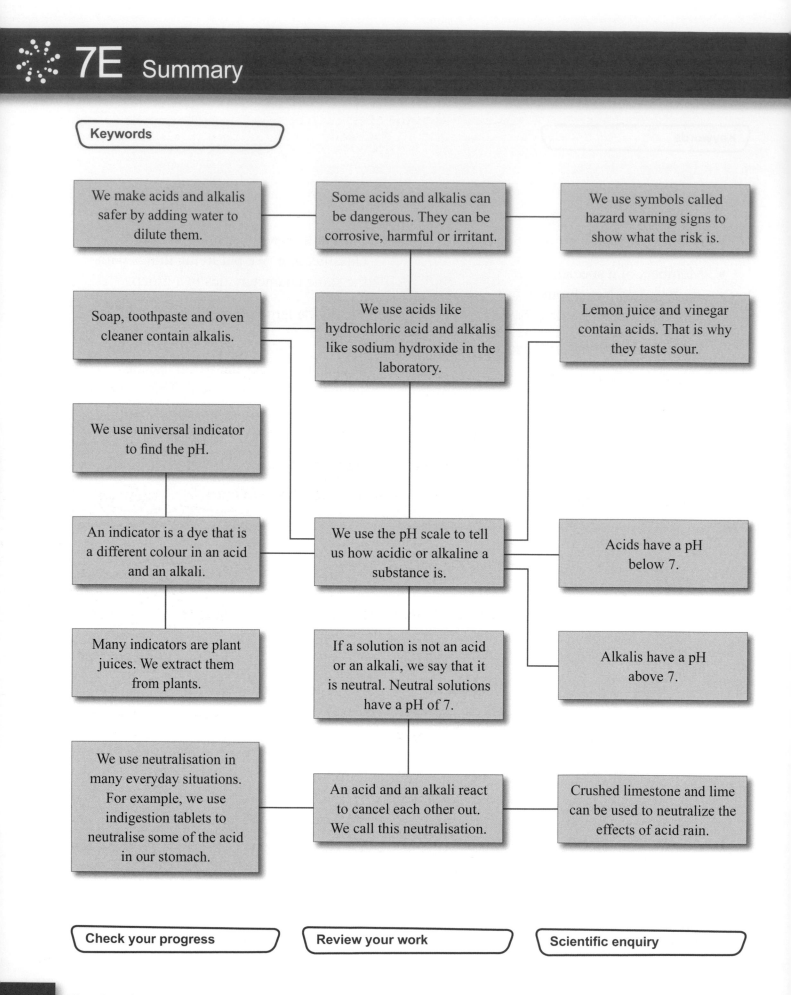

We make acids and alkalis safer by adding water to dilute them.

Some acids and alkalis can be dangerous. They can be corrosive, harmful or irritant.

We use symbols called hazard warning signs to show what the risk is.

Soap, toothpaste and oven cleaner contain alkalis.

We use acids like hydrochloric acid and alkalis like sodium hydroxide in the laboratory.

Lemon juice and vinegar contain acids. That is why they taste sour.

We use universal indicator to find the pH.

An indicator is a dye that is a different colour in an acid and an alkali.

We use the pH scale to tell us how acidic or alkaline a substance is.

Acids have a pH below 7.

Many indicators are plant juices. We extract them from plants.

If a solution is not an acid or an alkali, we say that it is neutral. Neutral solutions have a pH of 7.

Alkalis have a pH above 7.

We use neutralisation in many everyday situations. For example, we use indigestion tablets to neutralise some of the acid in our stomach.

An acid and an alkali react to cancel each other out. We call this neutralisation.

Crushed limestone and lime can be used to neutralize the effects of acid rain.

Check your progress

Review your work

Scientific enquiry

Keywords

Key ideas

- In a chemical reaction, new substances are produced.

- Substances that are used up in a chemical reaction are called reactants.

- Substances that are made during a chemical reaction are called products.

- Hydrogen is produced when an acid reacts with a metal. The metal is used up. We call this corrosion.

- When a metal and an acid react, they produce a salt as well as hydrogen.

- We test for hydrogen using a lighted splint. You hear a pop if there is hydrogen.

- An acid reacts with a carbonate to produce new substances. One of these is carbon dioxide.

- We use lime water to test for carbon dioxide. It is the only gas that turns lime water cloudy.

- Your body makes carbon dioxide through the process of respiration.

- When something burns, it reacts with oxygen.

- The oxide of a substance is made when a substance burns.

- Fuels release energy when they burn.

- A fire needs oxygen from air, fuel and heat to burn. We show this as a fire triangle.

- Fossil fuels come from the remains of plants and animals that died millions of years ago.

- Fossil fuels produce carbon dioxide and water when they burn.

- Coal, oil and petrol are examples of fossil fuels.

- Methane is an example of a fossil fuel. Its common name is natural gas.

- Carbon dioxide reacts with rainwater to make acid rain.

Check your progress   Review your work   Scientific enquiry

All the substances we can see and feel in the world are called matter.

Scientists look at what matter does. They think of ideas to explain what they see. These ideas are called theories.

Scientists think that all matter is made from very small particles.

The particles are so small that they are invisible.

The particles are always moving.

The particles are arranged in different ways in solids, liquids and gases.

Heat travels in solids by conduction. The vibration of the particles is passed through a solid as the particles knock into each other.

In liquids, the particles are still attracted to each other but they move faster. They swap places with each other. There is a little more space between the particles.

In a gas, there is little attraction between the particles so they move freely. The particles are far apart and moving very fast.

In solids, strong forces hold the particles together so they vibrate, but do not change places. There is little space between particles.

Solids and liquids are difficult to compress, but gases compress easily. This is because gases have large gaps between the particles.

Expansion means getting bigger. Solids expand slightly; liquids expand more and gases expand a great deal. During expansion the particles move further apart.

Solids don't flow because the forces between the particles are strong. Gases and liquids flow because the forces between particles are much weaker.

Substances can be sorted into three groups: solids, liquids and gases. These three groups are called the three states of matter.

If you heat a solid, the particles can break away from each other and the solid melts.

Heating particles in a liquid makes them escape as a gas. This is evaporation.

Particles spread out because they are moving We call this diffusion.

Keywords

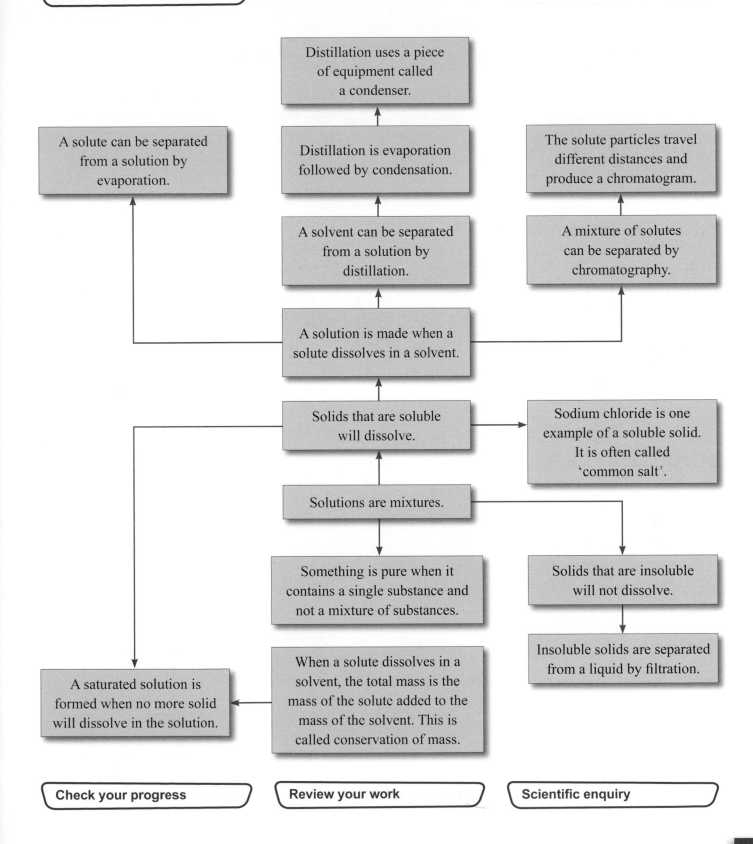

Distillation uses a piece of equipment called a condenser.

A solute can be separated from a solution by evaporation.

Distillation is evaporation followed by condensation.

The solute particles travel different distances and produce a chromatogram.

A solvent can be separated from a solution by distillation.

A mixture of solutes can be separated by chromatography.

A solution is made when a solute dissolves in a solvent.

Solids that are soluble will dissolve.

Sodium chloride is one example of a soluble solid. It is often called 'common salt'.

Solutions are mixtures.

Something is pure when it contains a single substance and not a mixture of substances.

Solids that are insoluble will not dissolve.

A saturated solution is formed when no more solid will dissolve in the solution.

When a solute dissolves in a solvent, the total mass is the mass of the solute added to the mass of the solvent. This is called conservation of mass.

Insoluble solids are separated from a liquid by filtration.

Check your progress

Review your work

Scientific enquiry

Key ideas

- We need energy to make things happen. It is measured in joules.

- There are different types of energy, such as kinetic energy and heat energy.

- Fuels are very important in our lives. We use many different fuels.

- The energy that fuels release is useful for transport, heating, cooking and making electricity.

- Fossil fuels are made from the remains of plants and animals that died millions of years ago.

- Fossil fuels will run out. They are non-renewable.

- We use fossil fuels to make most of our electricity.

- It is important to save fossil fuels because they are running out and because burning them contributes to acid rain and global warming.

- 1 kilojoule is 1000 joules.

- Renewable energy resources such as wind energy won't run out as long as the Sun keeps shining.

- Most renewable energy resources depend on the Sun.

- There are lots of renewable energy resources, such as solar energy and geothermal energy.

- Renewable energy resources do not cause air pollution.

- Animals eat food to get their energy. The energy in food is measured in kilojoules or kilocalories.

- Activities that we do all need energy. We get the energy we need from the chemical energy in food.

- Plants make food using the energy in sunlight.

- All the energy in food ultimately comes from the Sun.

- We need to match the energy in our diet to the energy our bodies need to keep a constant body weight.

Check your progress   Review your work   Scientific enquiry

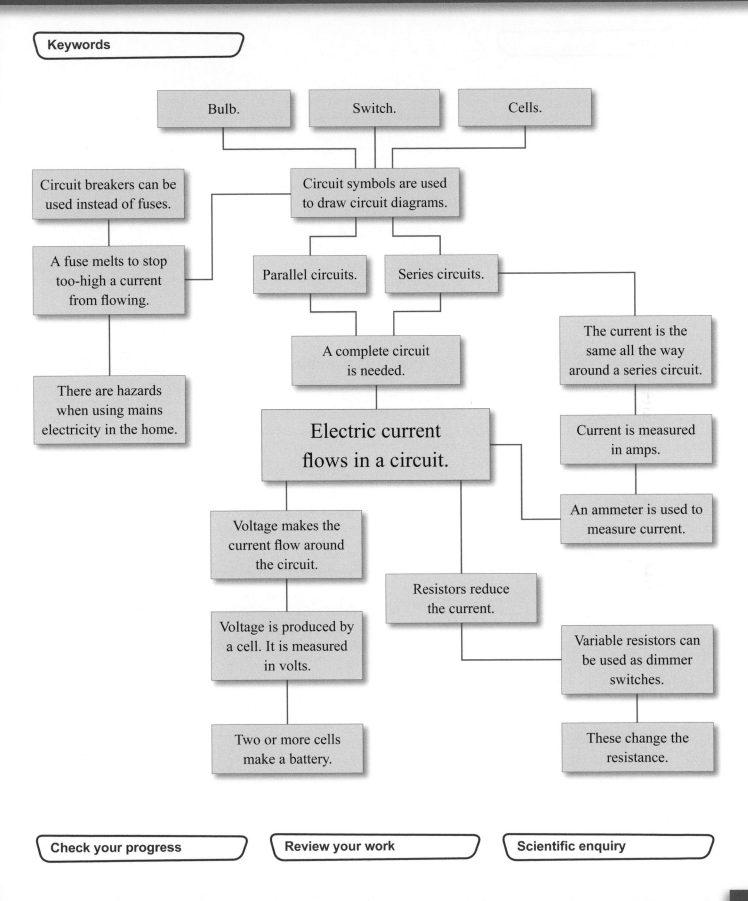

Bulb.

Switch.

Cells.

Circuit breakers can be used instead of fuses.

Circuit symbols are used to draw circuit diagrams.

A fuse melts to stop too-high a current from flowing.

Parallel circuits.

Series circuits.

The current is the same all the way around a series circuit.

A complete circuit is needed.

There are hazards when using mains electricity in the home.

Electric current flows in a circuit.

Current is measured in amps.

An ammeter is used to measure current.

Voltage makes the current flow around the circuit.

Resistors reduce the current.

Voltage is produced by a cell. It is measured in volts.

Variable resistors can be used as dimmer switches.

Two or more cells make a battery.

These change the resistance.

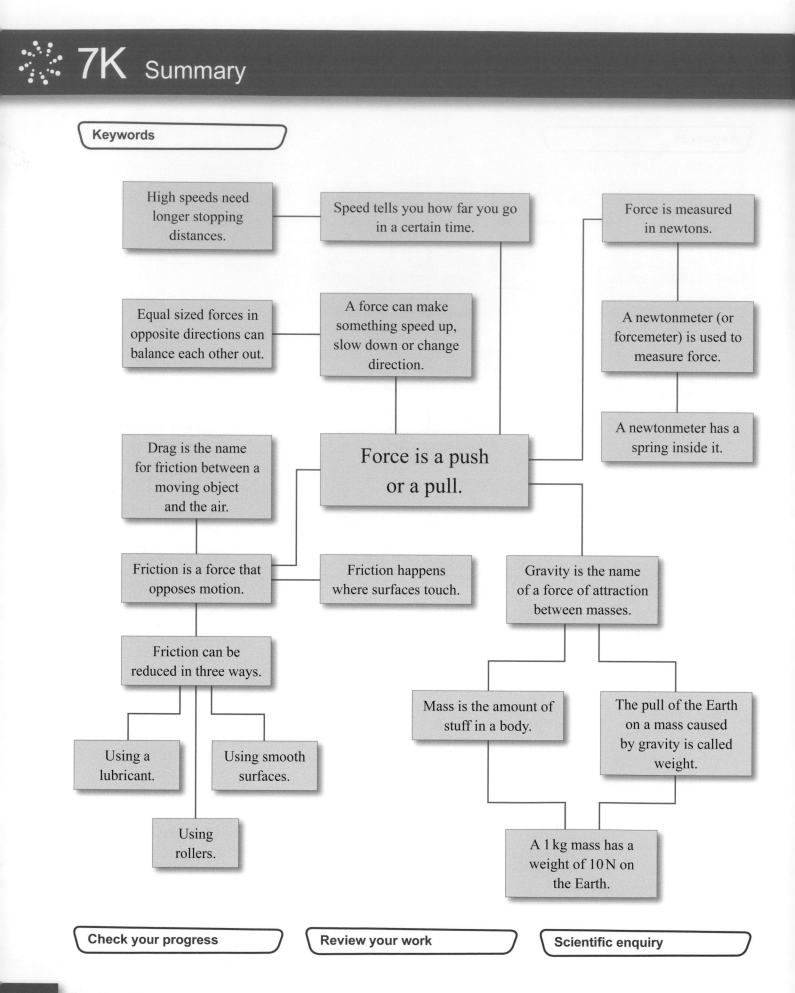

High speeds need longer stopping distances.

Speed tells you how far you go in a certain time.

Force is measured in newtons.

Equal sized forces in opposite directions can balance each other out.

A force can make something speed up, slow down or change direction.

A newtonmeter (or forcemeter) is used to measure force.

Drag is the name for friction between a moving object and the air.

Force is a push or a pull.

A newtonmeter has a spring inside it.

Friction is a force that opposes motion.

Friction happens where surfaces touch.

Gravity is the name of a force of attraction between masses.

Friction can be reduced in three ways.

Using a lubricant.

Using smooth surfaces.

Mass is the amount of stuff in a body.

The pull of the Earth on a mass caused by gravity is called weight.

Using rollers.

A 1 kg mass has a weight of 10 N on the Earth.

Check your progress

Review your work

Scientific enquiry

Key ideas

- A day is the time that the Earth takes to spin once around its axis.

- A year is the time that the Earth takes to orbit once around the Sun.

- Seasons happen because the Earth is tilted on its axis. When the northern hemisphere is tilted towards the Sun, it is summer there.

- The days are longer in summer because of the tilt of the Earth's axis.

- We see stars because they are luminous.

- The stars appear to move across the night sky because the Earth is rotating.

- We see the planets because they reflect the light from the Sun. They are non-luminous.

- The Moon reflects light from the Sun. The phases of the Moon are caused by only seeing the side of the Moon that is in the Sun's light as the Moon orbits the Earth.

- A solar eclipse happens when the Sun, Moon and Earth line up with the Moon in the middle.

- A lunar eclipse happens when the Sun, Moon and Earth line up with the Earth in the middle.

- Nine planets are recognised in the Solar System – Mercury, Venus, Earth, Mars, Jupiter, Saturn, Uranus, Neptune and Pluto.

- These nine planets orbit the Sun and their orbits take different times to complete.

- The asteroid belt is a group of rocks orbiting the Sun between Mars and Jupiter.

- The Earth is the only planet that we know of that has life on it.

Check your progress   Review your work   Scientific enquiry

Glossary/Index

Acknowledgements

Alamy 7D.HSWb (©Holt Studios International Ltd); **Allsport Concepts / Getty Images** 7G.3c (Chris Cole), 7K.4b (Gray Mortimore); **Andrew Lambert** 7E.5b; 7F.1c, 7F.1j, 7F.3a, 7J.HSWa, 7J.HSWe, 7J.HSWf; **Art Directors** 7A.2c, 7A.3a, 7A.3g, 7B.2c, 7B.5c, 7C.2a, 7D.1c, 7D.1d, 7D.1e, 7D.5d, 7F.1d, 7F.1f, 7F.1g, 7F.1i, 7F.4a, 7F.4b; **B&C Alexander** 7B.1d; **Biophoto Associates** 7B.4a; **Bruce Coleman Collection** 7C.1a, 7C.1b, 7C.2b, 7C.2c, 7C.2e; **Bubbles Photolibrary** 7B.5a (Jennie Woodcock), 7I.4a (Angela Hampton), 7I.4b (Jennie Woodcock), 7I.4d (Chris Rout); **Corbis** 7A.2b (Bettmann), 7B.HSW (O Franken), 7F.HSWa (Archivo Iconographico S.A.), 7K.HSWa (Sergio Pitaman), 7K.HSWc; **Dave Acaster** 7E.HSW; **Ecoscene** 7I.HSWa (Anthony Cooper), 7I.HSWb (Jon Winkley); **Grant Heilman** 7A.3f (Kent Wood); **Greg Evans Photo Library** 7D.1b, 7D.1f, 7D.1g; **IBM UK Labs** 7J.HSWc; **Ida Cook** 7F.1a, 7F.1b 7H.4a; **The Image Bank / Getty Images** 7G.3b (Patti McConville); **Janice Weidel** 7D.1a; **John Adds** 7A.3c; **Mary Evans Photo Library** 7D.2a, 7D.2b, 7D.2c; **Microscopix** 7A.2a (Andrew Syred); **NASA** 7L.5a; **National Maritime Musuem, London** 7K.HSWb; **Natural History Museum, London** 7D.HSWa; **naturepl. com** 7C.HSW (Kim Taylor); **NHPA / Photoshoot** 7C.1c (Micheal Tweedie), 7C.2d (Stephen Dalton), 7I.2a (Daniel Huedin); **Olivia Johnston** 7E.4a; **Oxford Scientific Films** 7B.1c (Michael Fogden), 7D.5b (Mark Hamblin), 7D.5c (Konrad Wothe), 7D.5e (David Tipling), 7D.5f (OSF), 7D.5g (OSF), 7D.5h (London Scientific Films); **Philip Harris Education** 7K.1a; **Science Photo Library** 7A.1a (Alfred Pasieka), 7A.3b (Dr Gopal Murti), 7A.3d (Astrid & Hans-Freide Michler), 7A.3e (Claud Nurilsang & Marc Perenou), 7A.HSWc (Dr Kari Lounatmaa), 7B.1a (D Philips), 7B.1b (CNRI), 7B.2a (CC Studios), 7B.2b (Gary Parker), 7B.5b (Mark Clarke), 7B.5d (Mark Clarke), 7D.1h (Peter Menzel), 7D.4a (Prof P Motta), 7D.5a (David Aubrey), 7E.5a (Prof. P. Motta), 7F.1e (Martin Bond), 7F.1h (Jerry Mason), 7F.HSWb (Andrew McCleanaghan), 7G.2a (Northwestern Univesity Library), 7G.3a (Martin Dohrn), 7G.HSWa, 7G.HSWb (US Library of Congress),7I.1a (David Duscros), 7I.1b (Jim Selby), 7I.1c (Alan & Sandy Carey), 7I.1d (Simon Fraser), 7I.1e (Deep Light Productions), 7I.1f (David Nunak), 7I.1g (Alan Sirulnikoff), 7I.1h (Martin Bond), 7I.2b (Mark Clarke), 7I.4c (Simon Fraser), 7I.4e (David Frazier/Agstock), 7J.HSWb (Maximilian Stock Ltd), 7J.HSWd (Sheila Terry), 7K.HSWd (John Howard), 7K.HSWb (US Library of Congress), 7L.3a (Pekka Parviainen), 7L.3b (John Sandford), 7L.4a (Dr Fred Espenak), 7L.4b (Dr Fred Espenak), 7L.HSW (Matthew Oldfield); **Still Pictures** 7E.5c (Mark Edwards); **The Dean and Chapter of York** 7F.3b, 7F.3c; **Vanessa Miles** 7H.2a, 7K.4a; **Wellcome Library** London 7A.2d, 7E.1a, 7A.HSW

Image references show the Unit and Topic of the book (eg. 7A.1) and the order of the image in the Topic from top to bottom, left to right (e.g. 7A.1b is the second photograph in Topic 1 of Unit 7A).

Series advisors Andy Cooke, Jean Martin
Series authors Sam Ellis, Jean Martin

Series consultants Diane Fellowes-Freeman, Richard Needham

Based on original material by Derek Baron, Trevor Bavage, Paul Butler, Andy Cooke, Zoe Crompton, Sam Ellis, Kevin Frobisher, Jean Martin, Mick Mulligan, Chris Ram